Popular Love Songs & Wedding Music

Arranged by DAN COATES

Project Manager: Carol Cuellar
Cover Design: Debbie Johns

Contents

ALWAYS

Written by
JONATHAN LEWIS, WAYNE LEWIS
and DAVID LEWIS
Arranged by DAN COATES

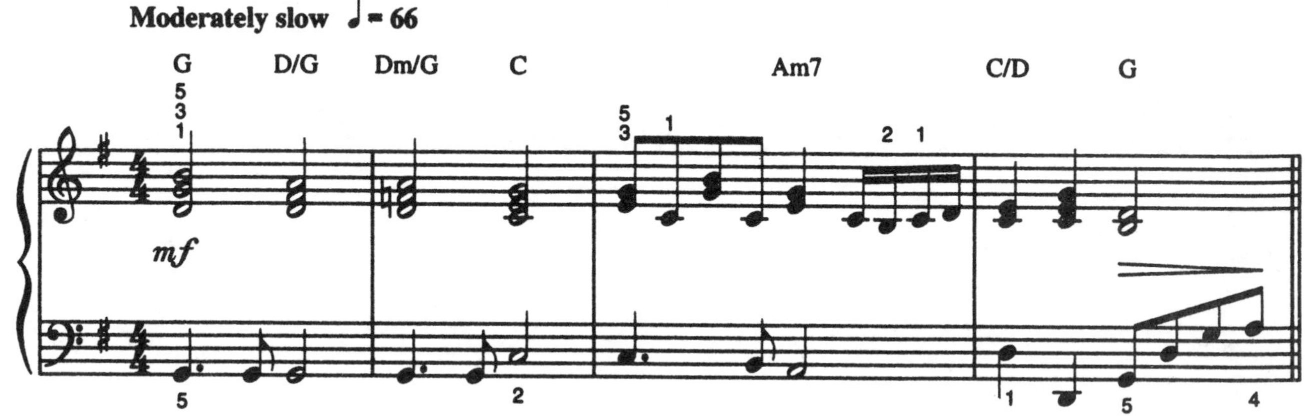
Moderately slow ♩ = 66
G D/G Dm/G C Am7 C/D G
mf

G D/G Dm/G C
Boy:
1. Girl, you are to me all ___ that a wo - man should be, and I
2. Come with me, my sweet; let's go make a fam - i - ly. And
mp

Am7 Am7/D G D/G
Girl:
ded - i - cate my life to you al - ways. A love like yours is rare; it
they will bring us joy for al - ways. Oh, boy, I love you so; I can't

G7
C
Am7
Am/D
G
Both:
must have been sent from up a - bove. And I
find e - nough ways to let you know. But you
know you'll stay this way for
can be sure I'm yours for
al - ways.
al - ways.
And

Cmaj7
Bm7
Cmaj7
Bm7 Am7 Bm7
we both
mf
know that our
love will
grow. And for -

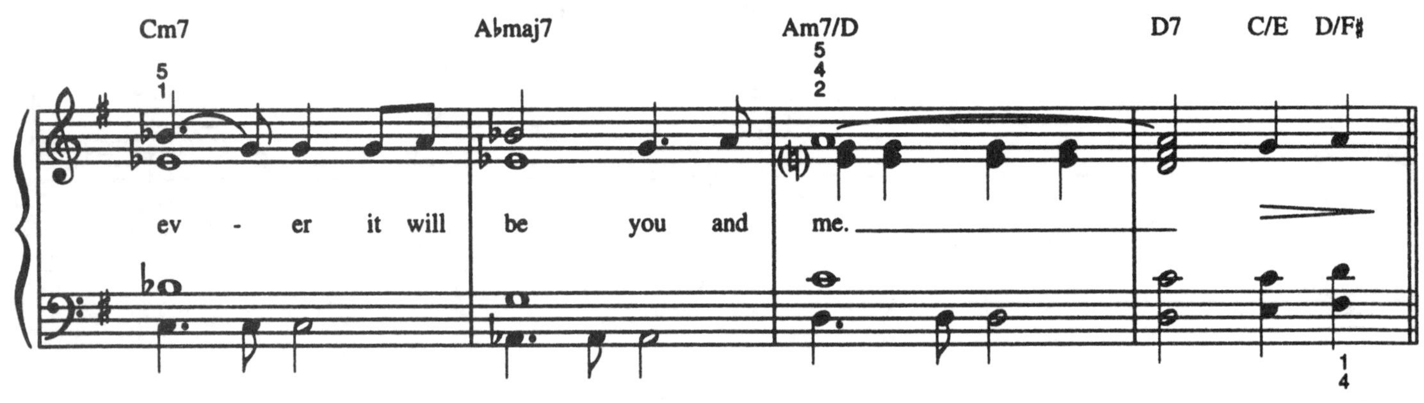
Cm7
A♭maj7
Am7/D
D7 C/E D/F♯
ev - er it will
be you and
me.

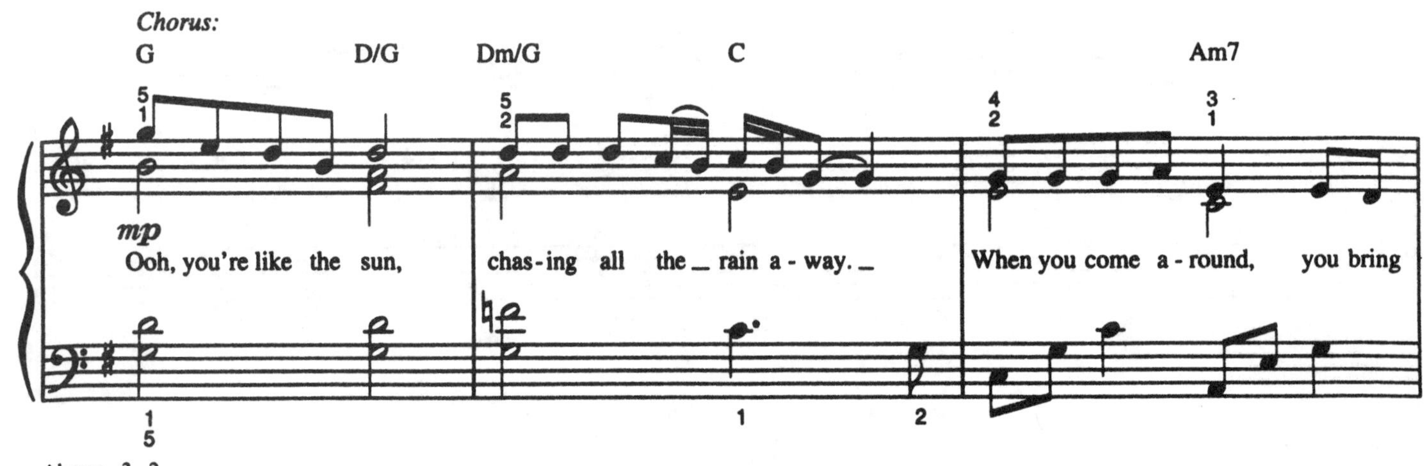
Chorus:
G
D/G
Dm/G
C
Am7
mp
Ooh, you're like the sun,
chas - ing all the rain a - way.
When you come a - round, you bring

Am/D G D/G Dm/G C
bright - er days. You're the pe - rfect one, for me, and you for-ev-er will be. And
mf

Am7
1.
Am/D G
2.
Am/D G
I will love you so for al - ways. al - ways.

G D/G Dm/G C Am7 Am/D G
Ooh ooh - hoo. I will love you so for al - ways.
mp

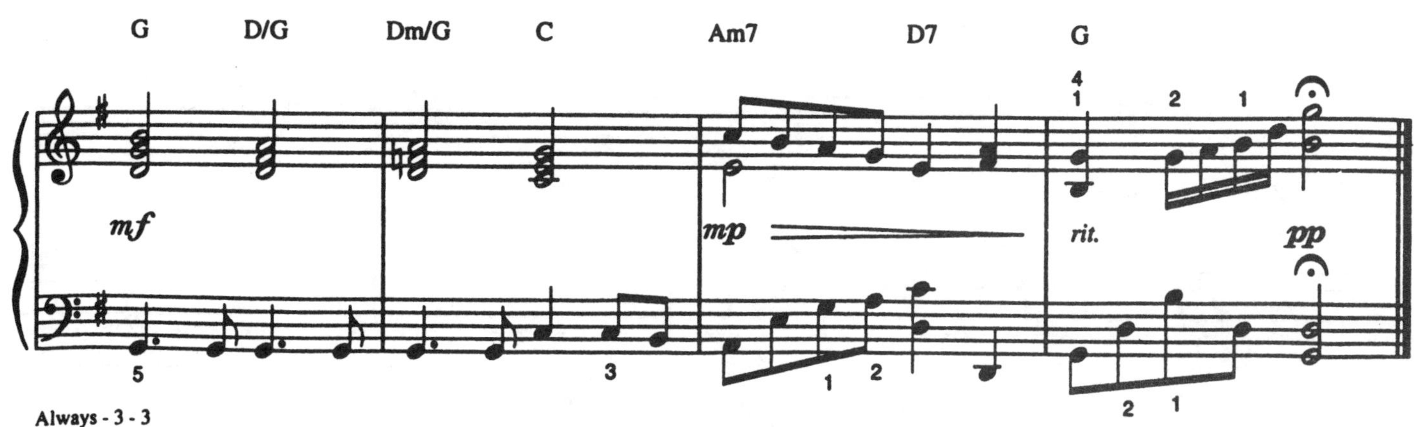
G D/G Dm/G C Am7 D7 G
mf
mp
rit.
pp

ANGEL EYES

Composed by
JIM BRICKMAN
Arranged by DAN COATES

F
G
C
G
Am
F
G
1
decresc.
F
G
Am
F
G
C
5
3
mp
F
G
Am
F
Em
Dm
5
5
3
cresc.
mf
3
1.
Dm7
3
G
5
1

2.
Dm7
G7sus4
G7
C
p
G
Am
F
G
C
mp
rit.
F
G
C
mf
a tempo
cresc.
f

BECAUSE YOU LOVED ME

(Theme from "UP CLOSE & PERSONAL")

Words and Music by
DIANE WARREN
Arrnaged by DAN COATES

Gm7/C
E♭
Dm7
be for - ev - er thank - ful, ba - by.
grate - ful for each day you gave me.
You're the one who held
May - be I don't know
mf
Gm7
me up,
that much, but I
nev - er let me fall.
know this much is true:
B♭m7
B♭/C
You're the one who saw me through,
I was blessed be - cause I was
through it all.
loved by you.
F
You were my
strength when I was weak,
you were my
mp

B♭
Dm
3
voice when I could - n't speak.
You were __ my
eyes when I could - n't see, __

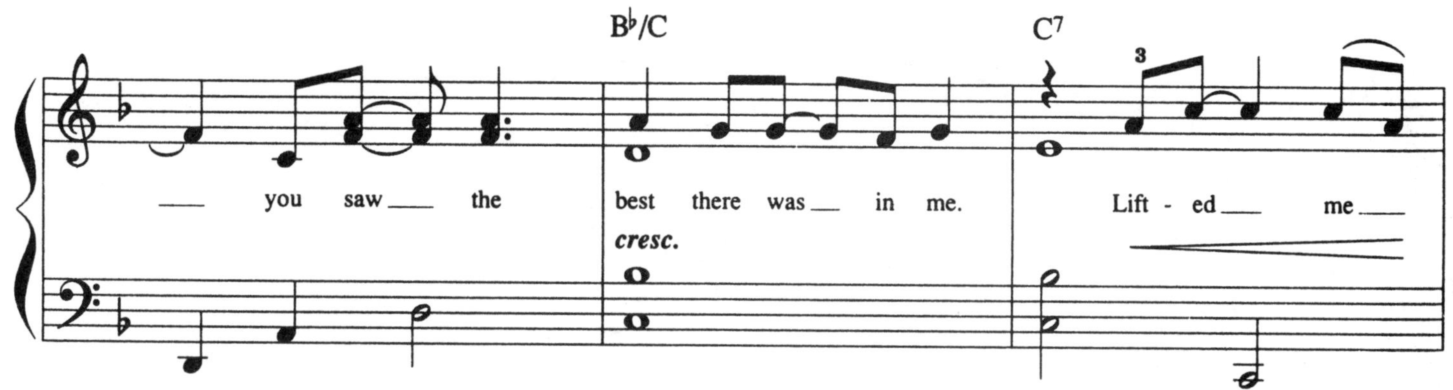
B♭/C
C7
3
__ you saw __ the
best there was __ in me.
Lift - ed __ me __
cresc.

Am7
B♭
E♭maj7
up when I could - n't reach,
you gave __ me
faith 'cause you __ be - lieved. __
mf

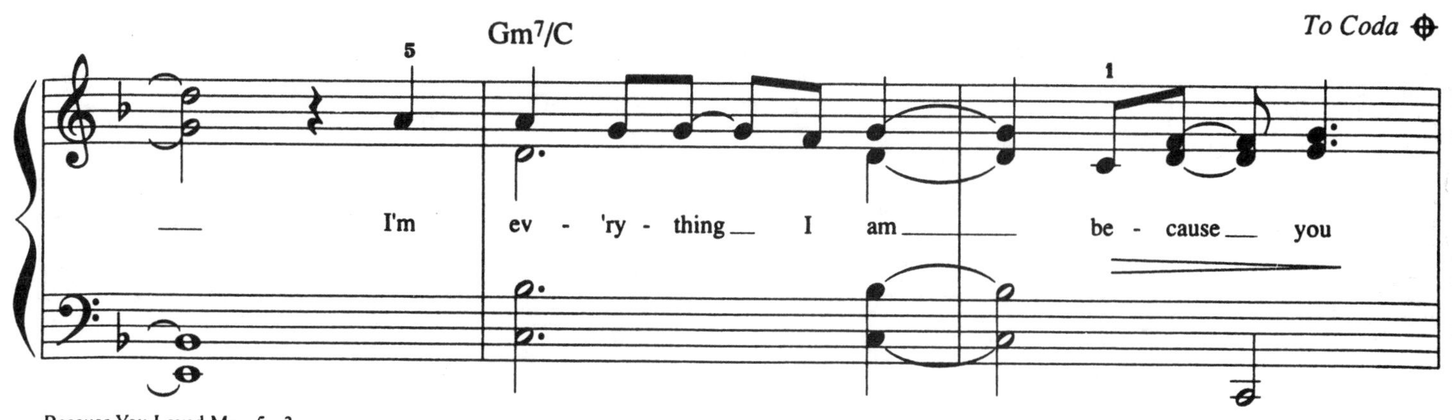
Gm7/C
To Coda
__ I'm
ev - 'ry - thing __ I am __
be - cause __ you

1.
F
B♭/C
loved me.
mp
2. You gave me
2.
F
A7
loved me.
mp
You were al - ways there
mf
Dm7
for me, the ten - der wind that car - ried me. A
A7
4
1
Dm
light in the dark,
shin- ing your love in - to my life.

Gm7
You've been my in - spi - ra - tion, through the
F/A
lies, you were the truth.
C7sus4
My world is a bet - ter place
be - cause of
B♭/C
you.
D.S. al Coda
You were my
Coda
F
loved me.
Gm7/C
I'm ev - 'ry - thing I am
be - cause you loved me.
F

BRIDAL CHORUS
(From "Lohengrin")

By
RICHARD WAGNER
Arranged by DAN COATES

mf
mp
cresc.
mf
D.S. al Fine

BUTTERFLY KISSES

Words and Music by
BOB CARLISLE and RANDY THOMAS
Arranged by DAN COATES

Dm7
C/E
F
Gsus4
G
F
G
she talks to Je - sus, and
I close my eyes. And I
thank God for all of the
C
F
F/G
joy in my life.
cresc.
Oh, but
most of all, for
Chorus:
C
but - ter - fly kiss - es af - ter
mf
bed - time prayer, stick - in'
G/C
Am
G
lit - tle white flow - ers all
up in her
hair.

F
C
"Walk be - side the po - ny, dad - dy, it's my first ride." "I
F
C
know the cake looks fun - ny, dad - dy, but I sure tried." Oh, with
F G C Dsus4 D
To Coda
all that I've done wrong, I must have done some - thing right to de - serve a
cresc.
F G7 1. C
hug ev - 'ry morn - ing and but - ter - fly kiss - es at night.
dim.
mp

2.
C
E♭
night.
All the pre - cious
time,
Dm
C
like the
wind, the years go
by.
Pre - cious but - ter -
D.S. al Coda
E♭
Dm
F
G
fly,
spread your wings and
fly.
Coda
F
G7
love ev - 'ry morn - ing and
but - ter - fly kiss - es.
I could - n't

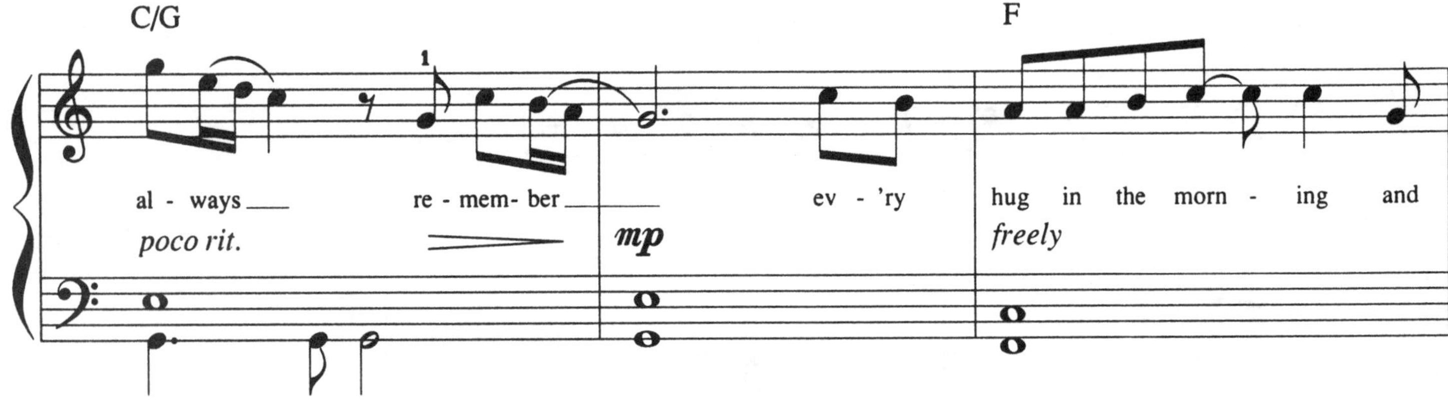

Verse 2:
Sweet sixteen today,
She's lookin' like her mama a little more every day.
One part woman, the other part girl;
To perfume and make-up from ribbons and curls.
Trying her wings out in a great big world.
But I remember:

Chorus 2:
Butterfly kisses after bedtime prayer,
Stickin' little white flowers all up in her hair.
"You know how much I love you, daddy, but if you don't mind,
I'm only gonna kiss you on the cheek this time."
Oh, with all that I've done wrong, I must have done something right
To deserve her love every morning
And butterfly kisses at night.

Verse 3:
She'll change her name today.
She'll make a promise, and I'll give her away.
Standing in the brideroom just staring at her,
She asks me what I'm thinking, and I say, "I'm not sure.
I just feel like I'm losing my baby girl."
Then she leaned over and gave me...

Chorus 3:
Butterfly kisses with her mama there,
Stickin' little white flowers all up in her hair.
"Walk me down the aisle, daddy, it's just about time."
"Does my wedding gown look pretty, daddy? Daddy, don't cry."
Oh, with all that I've done wrong, I must have done something right
To deserve her love every morning
And butterfly kisses. *(Coda)*

AMAZED

Words and Music by
MARV GREEN, AIMEE MAYO
and CHRIS LINDSEY
Arranged by DAN COATES

Gm
E♭
I can hear your thoughts,
I can see your dreams.

Chorus:
C
G
mf
I don't know how you do what you do.
I'm so in love with

Am
F
you.
It just keeps get - ting bet - ter.

C
G
I wan-na spend the rest of my life
with you by my side

Am
G
F
for - ev - er and ev - er.
E♭
F
Ev - 'ry lit - tle thing that you do, ba - by, I'm a - mazed by
1.
G
D
you. dim.
2.
G
B♭
C
you.
mf

G
B♭
F
C
Ev - 'ry lit - tle thing that you do,
G
I'm so in love with
Am
you. It just keeps get - ting bet -
F
ter.
C
I wan- na spend the rest of my life
G
with you by my side

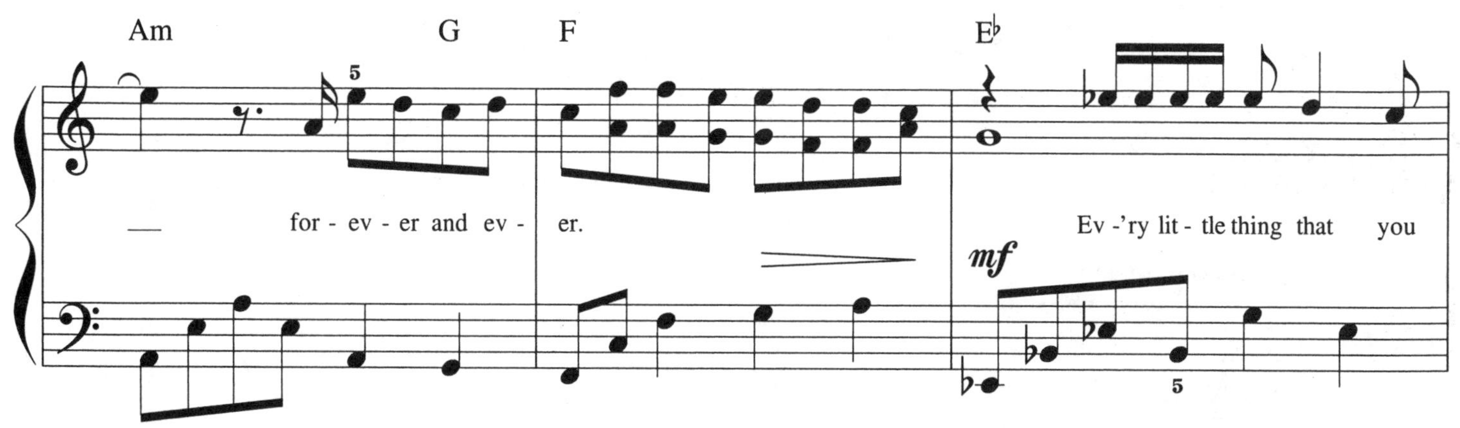

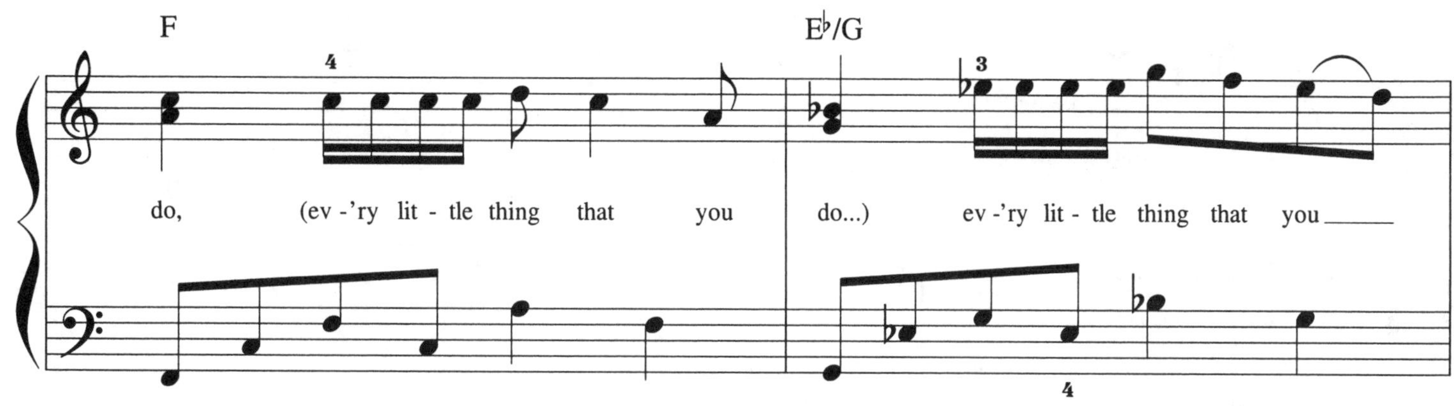

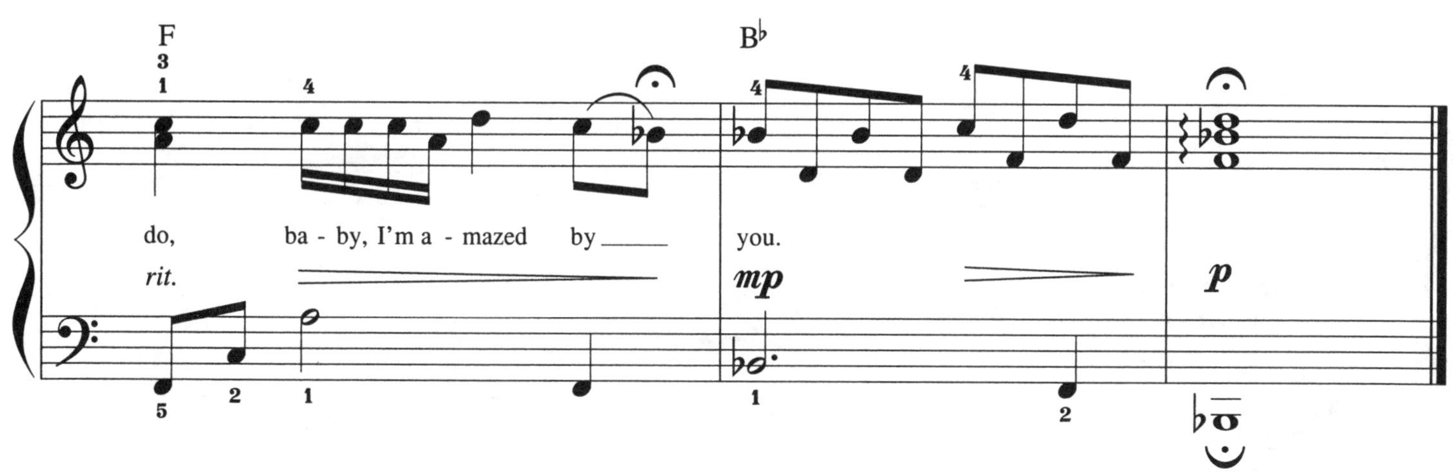

Verse 2:
The smell of your skin,
The taste of your kiss,
The way you whisper in the dark.
Your hair all around me,
Baby, you surround me.
You touch every place in my heart.
Oh, it feels like the first time every time.
I wanna spend the whole night in your eyes.
(To Chorus:)

COLORS OF THE WIND

(From Walt Disney's "POCAHONTAS")

Lyrics by
STEPHEN SCHWARTZ

Music by
ALAN MENKEN
Arranged by DAN COATES

D
Bm
D
think the on - ly peo - ple who are
rain - storm and the riv - er are my
peo - ple are the
broth - ers; the
peo - ple who look and think like
her - on and the ot - ter are my
F♯m
Bm
G
D
you, but
friends; and
if you walk the foot - steps of a
we are all con - nect - ed to each
strang - er you'll learn
oth - er in a
Em7
A7
1.
D
Bm
things you nev - er knew you nev - er
cir - cle, in a hoop that nev - er
knew. Have you
ev - er heard the wolf cry to the
mf
F♯m
G
Bm
F♯m
blue corn moon, or
asked the grin - ning bob - cat why he
grinned? Can you

G A D/F♯ Bm G
sing with all the voic - es of the moun - tain? Can you paint with all the col - ors of the
Bm7 Em7 A7 D
wind? Can you paint with all the col - ors of the wind?
mp
Bm D Bm
mp
Come
2.
D F♯m G F♯m Bm
ends. How high does the syc - a - more grow? If you
mf
C G/A A
cut it down, then you'll nev - er know. And you'll
rall.

Bm
F♯m
G
Bm
nev - er hear the wolf cry to the
blue corn moon,
for
wheth - er we are white or cop - per -
f a tempo
F♯m
G
A
D/F♯
Bm
skinned,
we need to
sing with all the voic - es of the
moun - tain,
need to
G
Bm
Em
A
paint with all the col - ors of the
wind.
You can
own the earth and still all you'll
mf
F♯m
G
Bm
G
A7
D
own is earth un - til you can
paint with all the col - ors of the
wind.
rit.
a tempo
Bm
G
A7
D
mp rall.
p

DREAMING OF YOU

Words and Music by
TOM SNOW and
FRAN GOLDE
Arranged by DAN COATES

G/B C Am7 Bm7(♭5) Cmaj7
you to - night. Till to - mor - row, I'll be hold - ing you tight. And there's
you to - night, till to - mor - row, and for all of my life. And there's
Am D/F♯ G C/E F
no - where in the world I'd rath - er be than
no - where in the world I'd rath - er be than
To Coda
Dm7 C/E F Gsus4 C B♭maj7/C
here in my room, dream - ing a - bout you and me.
here in my room, dream - ing with you, end - less -
Cmaj7 F B♭maj7 F/A G/B Cmaj7 F B♭maj7
2.Won - der if you ev - er see me and I won - der if you know I'm there.
3. I just wan - na hold you close, but so far all I have are dreams of you.
mp

C
Am7
Em
Am7
Em
If you looked in my eyes, would you see what's in - side? Would you
So, I wait for the day and the cour - age to say how much
G/B
C
1. F/A
G
2. F
G
e - ven care?
I love you.
Yes, I do. I'll be
C/E
F
G/B
C
Am7
dream - ing of you to - night. Till to - mor - row, I'll be
mf
Bm7(♭5)
Cmaj7
Am
D/F♯
G
C/E
hold - ing you tight. And there's no - where in the world I'd rath - er

F
Dm7
C/E
F
Gsus4
be than here in my room, dreaming about you and
C
Gm7
Bbmaj7
C
me.
mf
I can't stop dream - ing.
D.S. al Coda
Gm7
G7/B
C
Dm7
G7
I can't stop dream- ing of you.
Coda
C
Dm7
G7
C
Bb/C
ly.
mp
Dream- ing with you, end - less - ly.
rit. e dim.
p

FOR YOU I WILL

Words and Music by
DIANE WARREN
Arranged by DAN COATES

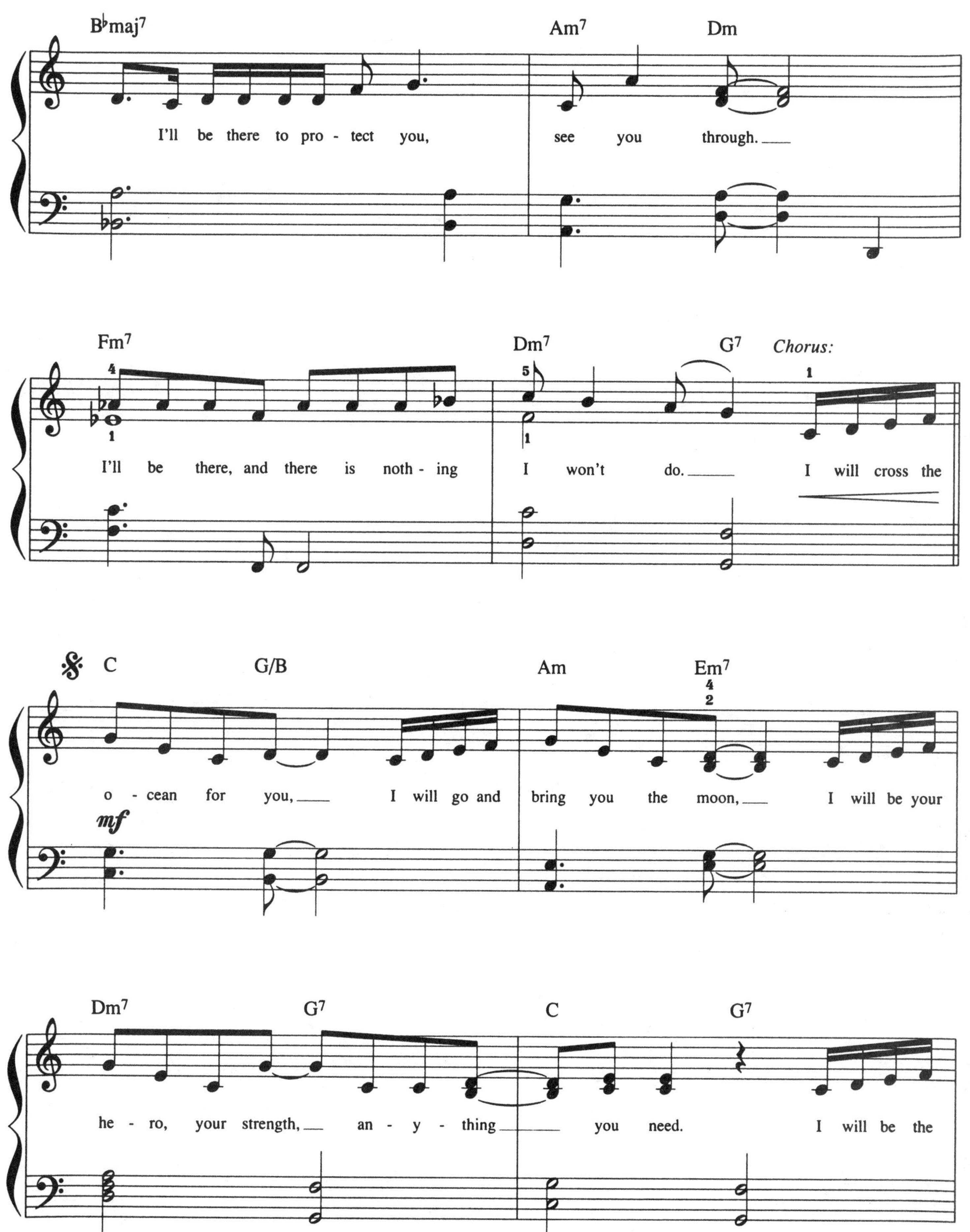
B♭maj7
I'll be there to pro - tect you,
Am7
Dm
see you through.
Fm7
I'll be there, and there is noth - ing
Dm7
G7
Chorus:
I won't do.
I will cross the
C
G/B
o - cean for you,
I will go and
mf
Am
Em7
bring you the moon,
I will be your
Dm7
G7
he - ro, your strength,
an - y - thing
C
G7
you need.
I will be the

C
G/B
Am7
Em7
sun in your sky, I will light your way for all time, promise
Dm
G7
To Coda
1.
C
G7sus4
G7
you, for you I will.
2. I will shield your
mp
2.
C
B♭
F/A
C
will.
For you, I will lay my life on the line.
mp
mf
E/G♯
Am7
Dm
C/E
For you, I'll fight, for you, I will die. With ev - 'ry breath, with all my soul, I
cresc.

D.S. 𝄋 al Coda
E7
Am
Fm7
G7
give my word, I'll give it all.
Put your faith in me,
I'll do an - y - thing. I will cross the
f
C
Dm
G7
Coda
will.
Prom - ise
you,
for you I
mp
C
Dm
G7
C
will.
I prom - ise
you,
for you I
will.
rit. e dim.
p

Verse 2:
I will shield your heart from the rain,
I won't let no harm come your way.
Oh, these arms will be your shelter,
No, these arms won't let you down.
If there is a mountain to move,
I will move that mountain for you.
I'm here for you, I'm here forever.
I will be a fortress, tall and strong.
I'll keep you safe, I'll stand beside you,
Right or wrong. *(To Chorus:)*

FOREVER'S AS FAR AS I'LL GO

Words and Music by
MIKE REID
Arranged by DAN COATES

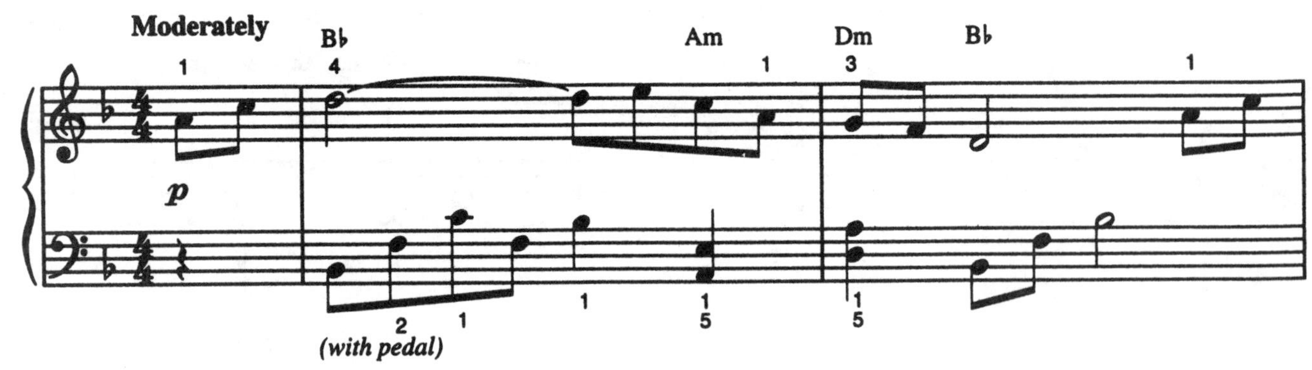

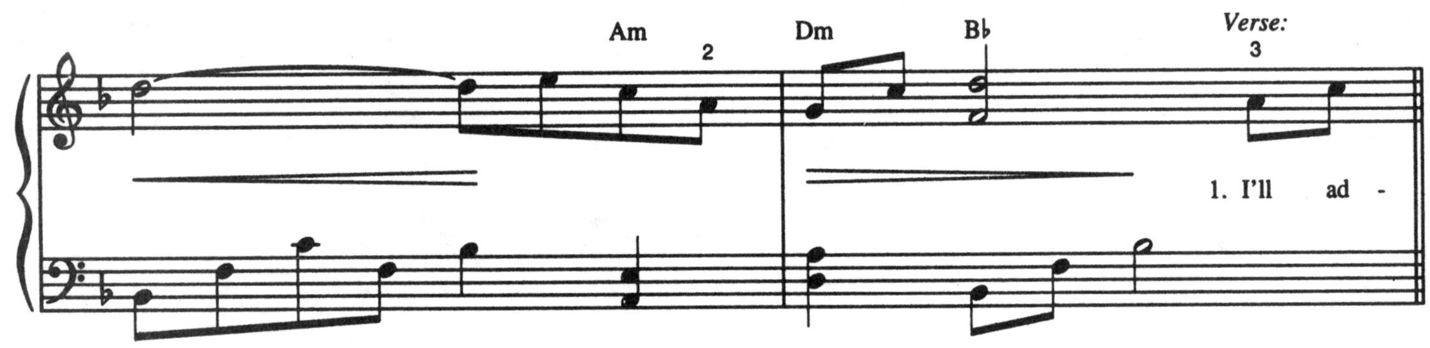

Chorus:
B♭6
B♭/C
C7
B♭/C
C
F/A
It's best that you know
where you stand with me.
I will

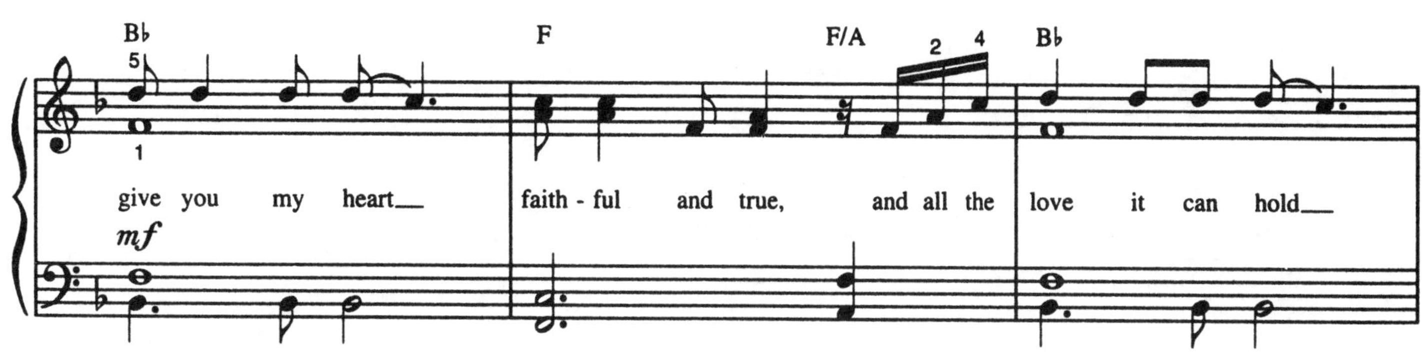
B♭
F
F/A
B♭
give you my heart
mf
faith - ful and true,
and all the
love it can hold

Am
Am7
Dm
Am7
B♭
that's all I can do.
But I've thought a - bout how
long I'll love you,

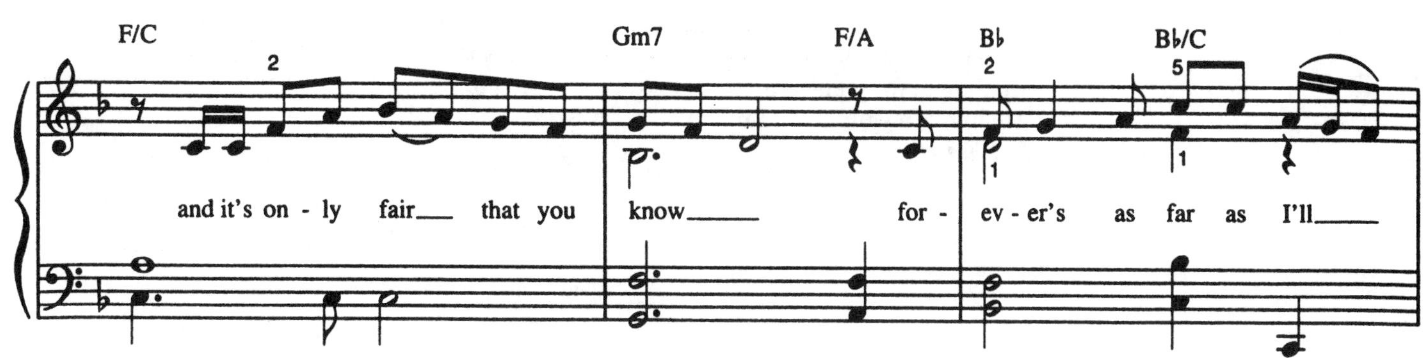
F/C
Gm7
F/A
B♭
B♭/C
and it's on - ly fair that you
know
for -
ev - er's as far as I'll

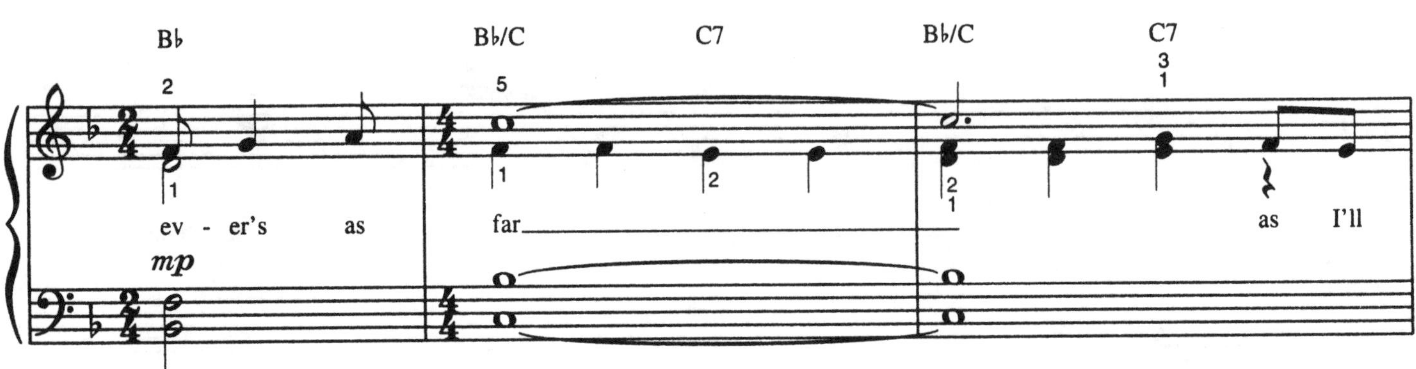

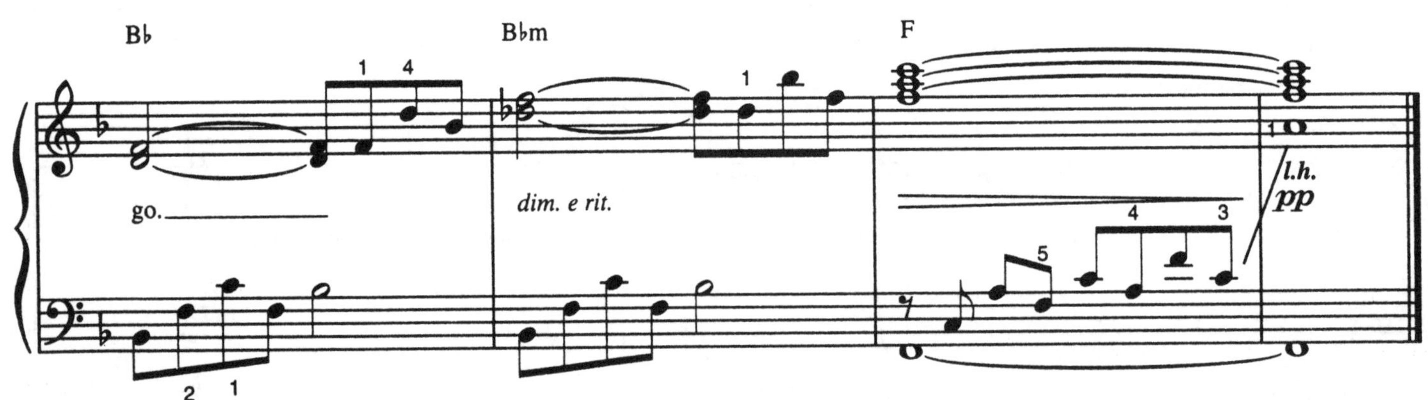

Verse 2:
When there's age around my eyes and gray in your hair,
And it only takes a touch to recall the love we've shared.
I won't take for granted that you know my love is true.
Each night in your arms, I will whisper to you...
(To Chorus:)

FOR YOUR EYES ONLY

Lyrics by MICHAEL LEESON
Music by BILL CONTI
Arranged by DAN COATES

E♭maj7
E♭/F
I never felt until I looked at you.
But you won't need to read between the lines.

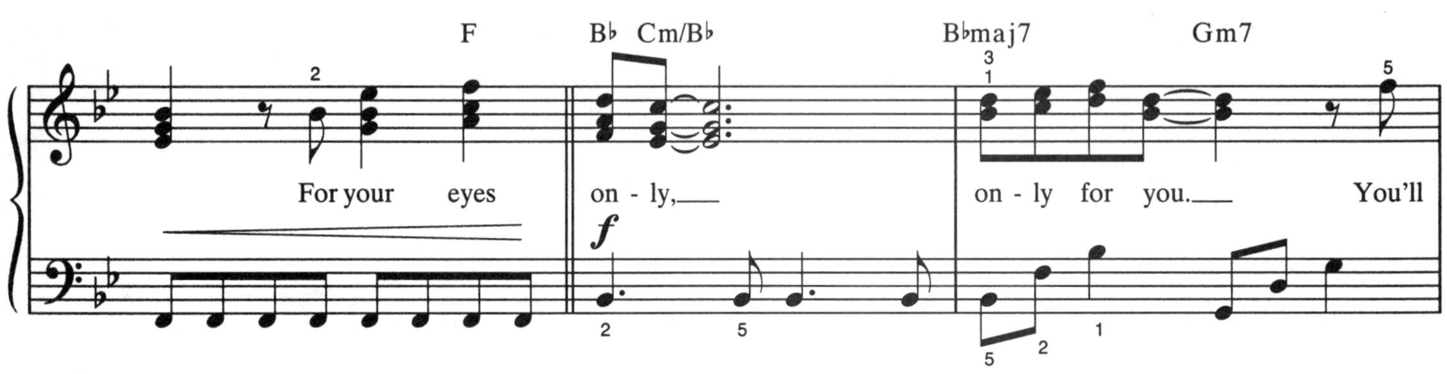
F
B♭ Cm/B♭
B♭maj7
Gm7
For your eyes only, only for you. You'll

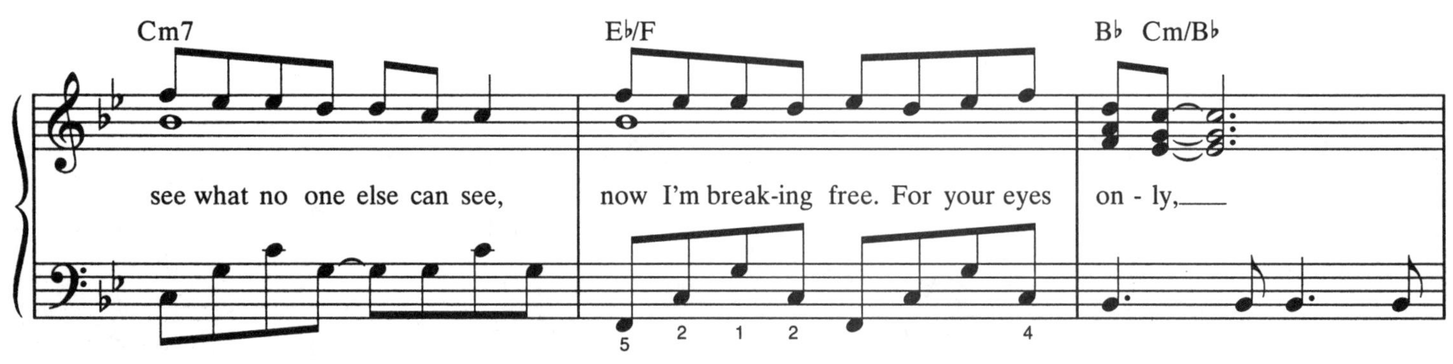
Cm7
E♭/F
B♭ Cm/B♭
see what no one else can see, now I'm breaking free. For your eyes only,

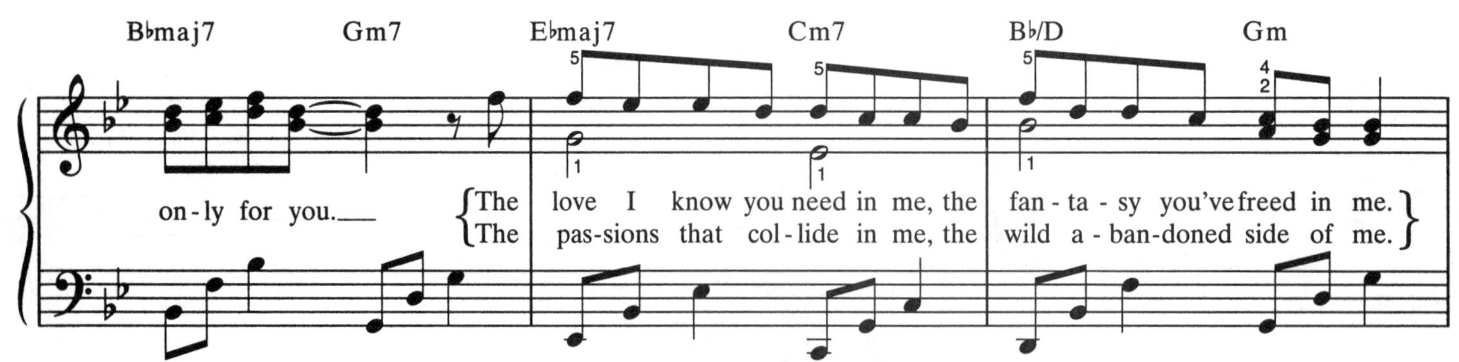
B♭maj7
Gm7
E♭maj7
Cm7
B♭/D
Gm
only for you. The love I know you need in me, the fantasy you've freed in me.
The passions that collide in me, the wild abandoned side of me.

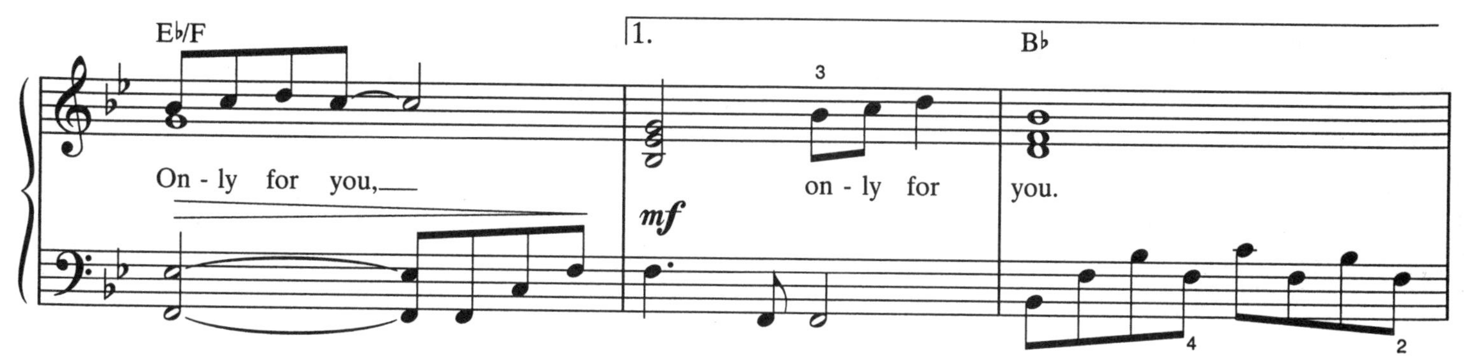
E♭/F
1.
B♭
On - ly for you,
on - ly for
you.
mf

8va
dim.
2. For

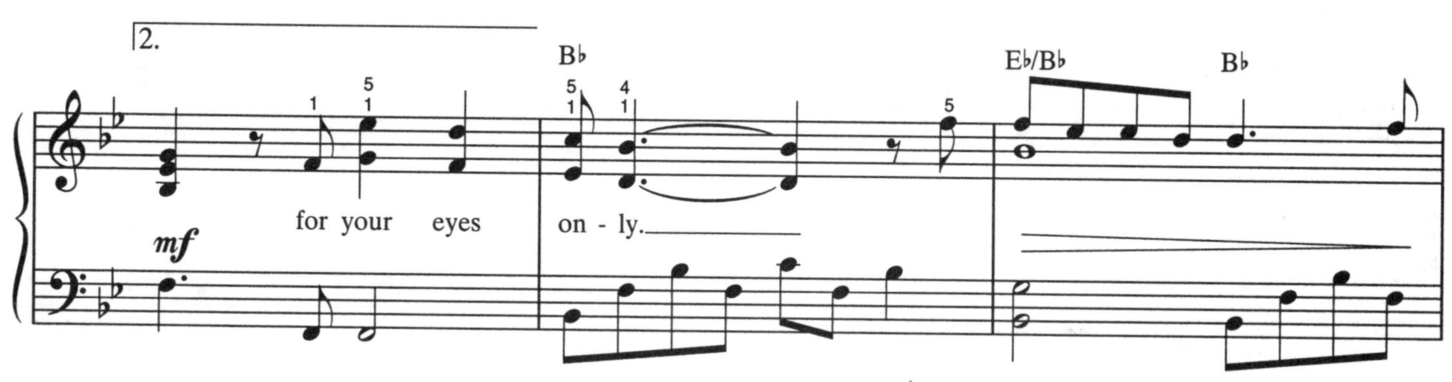
2.
B♭
E♭/B♭
B♭
mf
for your eyes
on - ly.

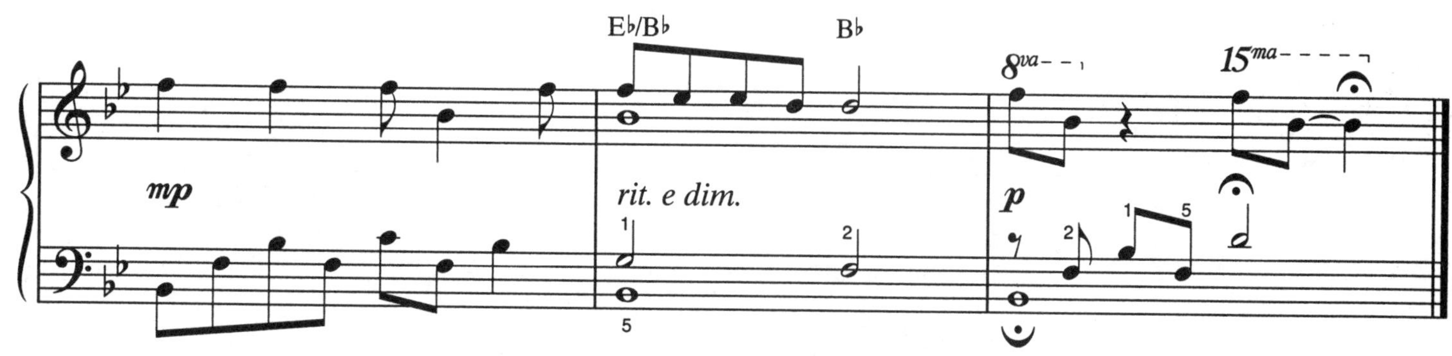
E♭/B♭
B♭
8va
15ma
mp
rit. e dim.
p

From the Motion Picture "THE PREACHER'S WIFE"

I BELIEVE IN YOU AND ME

Words and Music by
SANDY LINZER and DAVID WOLFERT
Arranged by DAN COATES

Am7
Gm7
C7
me. Oh, yes, you
will. And I be - lieve in
F
F7
B♭maj7
dreams a - gain. I be - lieve that
love will nev - er end. And
like the riv - er finds the
mf
B♭m7
E♭7
F/C
Am7
Dm7
sea, I was
lost, now I'm
free, 'cause
Gm7
B♭/C
1.
F
B♭/C
I be - lieve in you and
me.
2. I will nev - er

2.
F
Am7
Dm7
Am7
Dm7
me.
May - be I'm a fool to feel the way I do.
mf
Gm7
C7sus4
I would play the fool for - ev - er just to be with you for - ev - er.
C/D
D7
G
I be - lieve in mir - a - cles, and love's a
cresc.
f
G7
Cmaj7
E♭/F
A/C♯
mir - a - cle. And yes, ba - by, you're my dream come true. I was
G/D
Bm7
Em7
Am7
Am7/D
lost, now I'm free, oh, ba - by, 'cause I be - lieve in you and

Verse 2:
I will never leave your side,
I will never hurt your pride.
When all the chips are down,
I will always be around
Just to be right where you are, my love.
Oh, I love you, boy.
I will never leave you out,
I will always let you in
To places no one has ever been.
Deep inside, can't you see?
I believe in you and me.

From the Warner Bros. Film "PURE COUNTRY"

I CROSS MY HEART

Words and Music by
STEVE DORFF and ERIC KAZ
Arranged by DAN COATES

F
G
Dm7
feel it from — my — heart. From here on
C/E
F
G
af - ter, — let's stay the way we are — right — now. And share
Dm7
C/E
B♭
all the love and laugh - ter — that a life - time —
G7sus
G7
F/G
G7
— will al - low.
C
C/E
F
G
f
I cross my heart and prom - ise

C C/E F
to give all I've got to give to make
G7sus G7 C C C/E
all your dreams come true. In all the
F G G/F C/E
world you'll nev - er find
To Coda
F C/E Dm7 G7 1. C
a love as true as mine.
mp
F C/E Dm7 G7

C
2. C
2. You will
mine.
mp
And if a -
F
C/E
long the way we
find a day
mf
Dm7
G7
C
E♭
it starts to
storm, you've got the
prom - ise of my
D.S. 𝄋 al Coda 𝄌
B♭/D
Cm7
F7sus
F7
G7sus
G7
love to
keep you
warm.

Additional Lyrics

2. You will always be the miracle
   That makes my life complete.
   And as long as there's a breath in me
   I'll make yours just as sweet.
   As we look into the future,
   It's as far as we can see.
   So let's make each tomorrow
   Be the best that it can be.
   (To Chorus)

I DO

Words and Music by
PAUL BRANDT
Arranged by DAN COATES

Am G C F G Em F
You'll find the an - swer's still the same, it won't change from day to day for worse or
G Chorus: C G7 Am G F G
bet - ter. Will I promise - ise to be your best freind? And
cresc.
mf
C G7 Am G F G Em F
am I here un - til the end? Can I be sure I have been
C G Em F Em F
wait - in' for you? And did I say my love is true? Ba - by, I

Verse 3:
I know the time will disappear,
But this love we're building on will always be here.
No way that this is sinking sand,
On this solid rock we'll stand forever.
(To Chorus:)

I'LL BE THERE FOR YOU
(Theme From "Friends")

Words by
DAVID CRANE, MARTA KAUFFMAN,
ALLEE WILLIS, PHIL SOLEM and DANNY WILDE

Music by
MICHAEL SKLOFF
Arranged by DAN COATES

Am
G
al - ways stuck ___ in sec - cond gear, ___ and it
warned you there'd ___ be days like these. ___ But she
F
C
Dsus4
has - n't been ___ your day, your week, ___ your month, or ev - en your
did - n't tell ___ you when the world ___ has brought you down to your
cresc. poco a poco
D
G
C
year. But
knees, that
I'll ___ be there for ___ you ___
f
D
G
___ when the rain starts ___ to fall. I'll ___ be

C
D
2
there
for
you
like
I've
been
there
be -
G
1
C
D
fore.
I'll
be
there
for
you
'cause
you're
To Coda
1.
3
1
4
2
F
5
1
there
for
me,
too.
mf
2.
G
1

C
3
No one could ev - er know me, no one could ev
mf
- er see me
Em
3
since you're the on - ly one who
knows what it's like to be me.
Am
4
1
Some - one to face
the day with,
C/G
make it through all the rest with,

F
C/E
D
C/E
D
some - one I'll al - ways laugh with.
Ev - en at my worst, I'm best with
Em
C
D
you.
G
C
D
D.S. al Coda
Coda
G
C
I'll be there for you

D
G
when the
rain
starts
to
fall.
I'll
be
C
D
there
for
you
like
I've
been
there
be -
G
C
D
fore.
I'll
be
there
for
you
'cause
you're
F
G
there
for
me,
too.
rit. e dim.
mf

I LOVE YOU ALWAYS FOREVER

Words and Music by
DONNA LEWIS
Arranged by DAN COATES

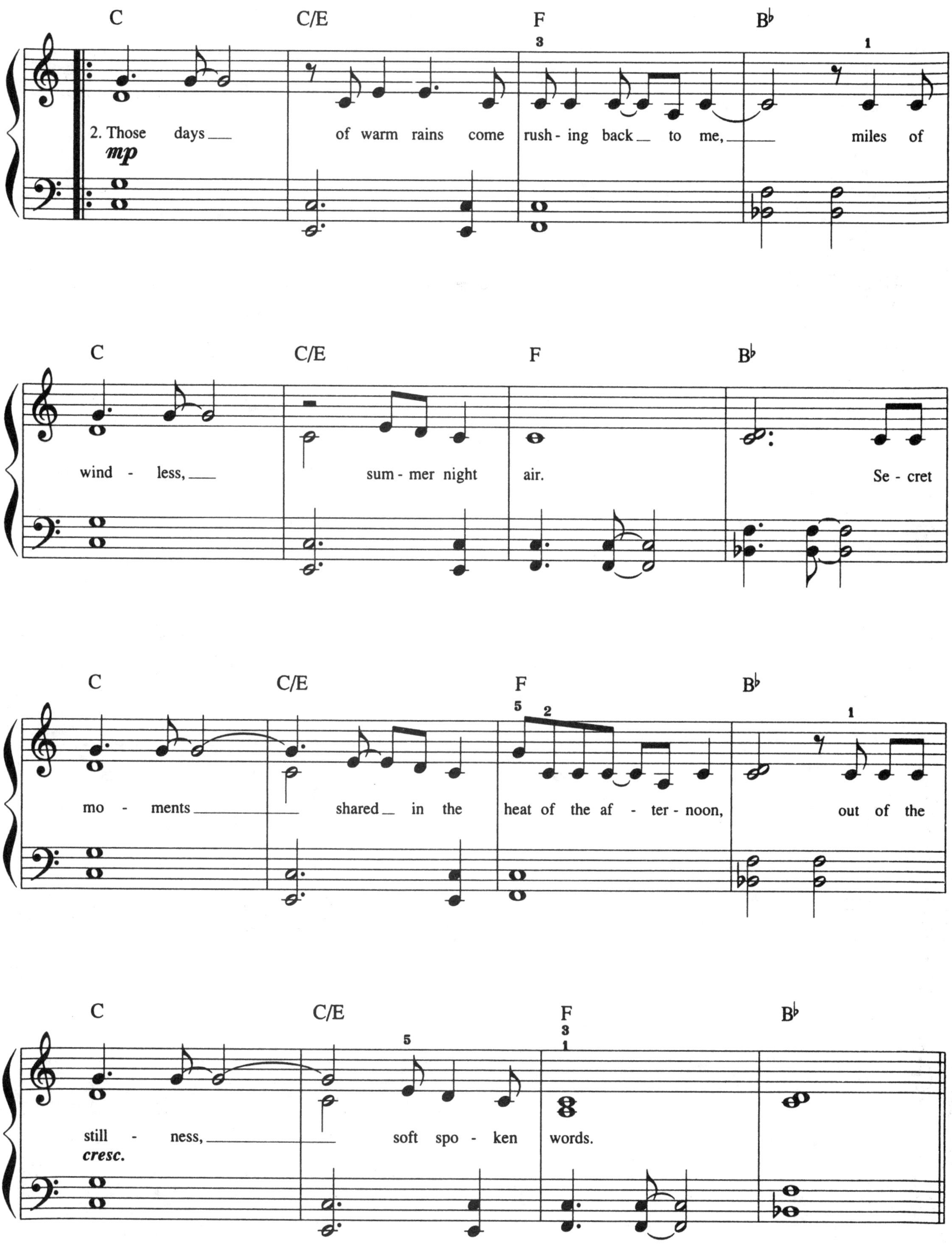

C C/E F B♭
2. Those days of warm rains come rush-ing back to me, miles of
mp
C C/E F B♭
wind - less, sum - mer night air. Se - cret
C C/E F B♭
mo - ments shared in the heat of the af - ter - noon, out of the
C C/E F B♭
still - ness, soft spo - ken words.
cresc.

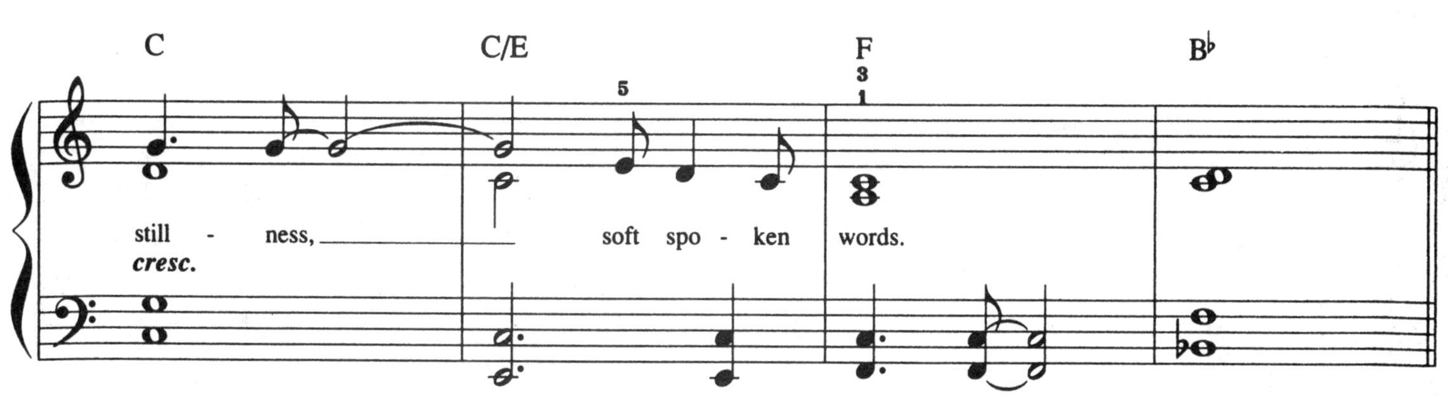

Chorus:

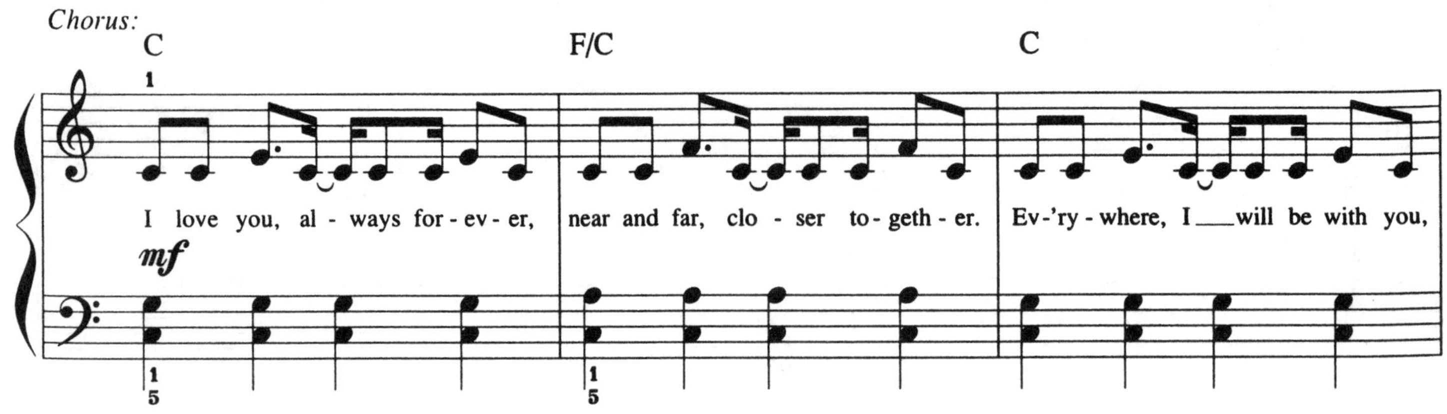
C
F/C
C
1
I love you, al - ways for - ev - er,
near and far, clo - ser to - geth - er.
Ev - 'ry - where, I will be with you,
mf
1
5
1
5

F/C
C
F/C
ev - 'ry - thing, I will do for you.
I love you, al - ways for - ev - er,
near and far, clo - ser to - geth - er.

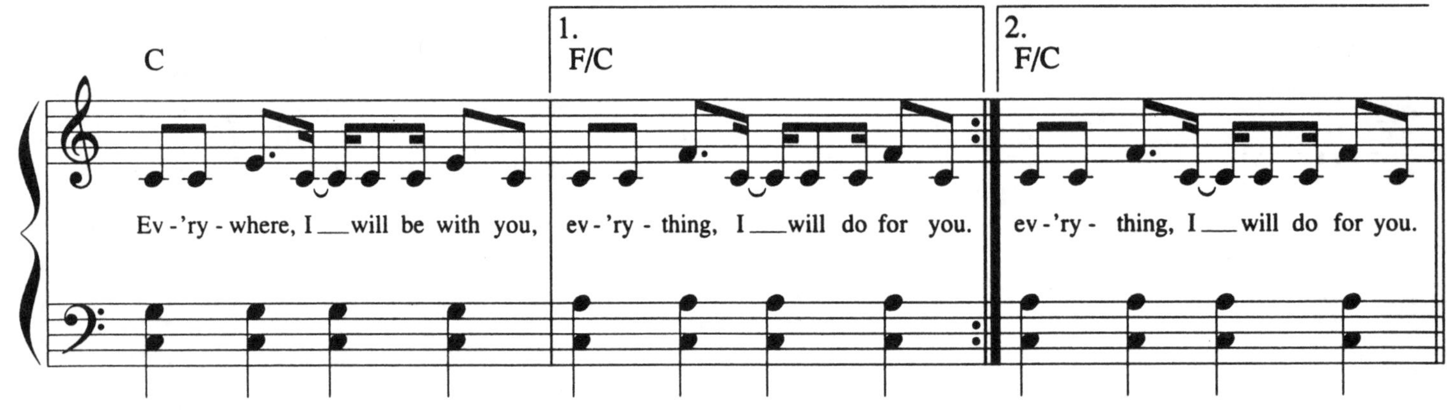
C
1.
F/C
2.
F/C
Ev - 'ry - where, I will be with you,
ev - 'ry - thing, I will do for you.
ev - 'ry - thing, I will do for you.

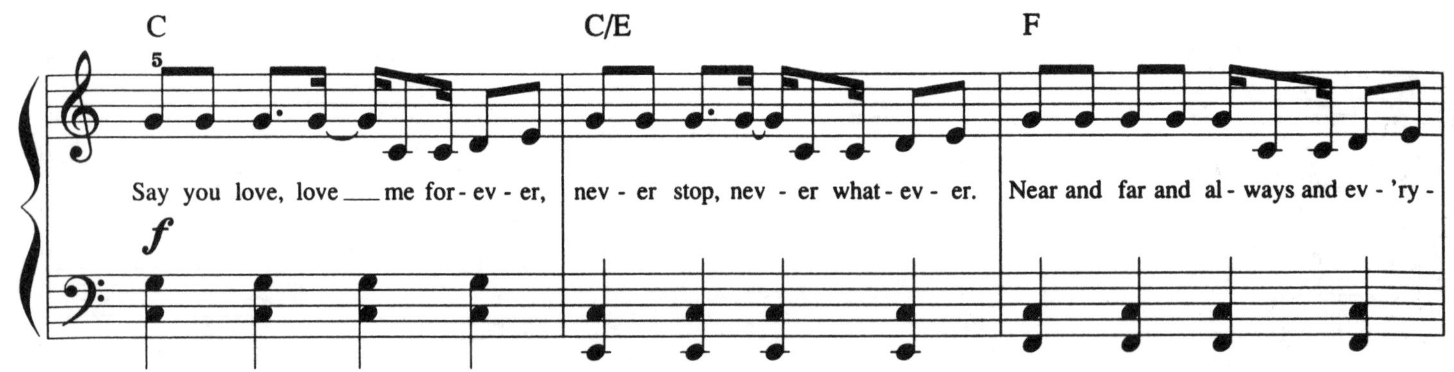
C
C/E
F
5
Say you love, love me for - ev - er,
nev - er stop, nev - er what - ev - er.
Near and far and al - ways and ev - 'ry -
f

Verse 3:
You've got the most unbelievable blue eyes I've ever seen.
You've got me almost melting away as we lay there
Under blue sky with pure white stars,
Exotic sweetness, a magical time.
(To Chorus:)

I SWEAR

Words and Music by
GARY BAKER and FRANK MYERS
Arranged by DAN COATES

F G7 C
I know my part. 'Cause I'll stand be - side
'ries on the wall. And when there's sil -
F/A G/B C F G
you through the years, you'll on - ly cry those hap - py tears.
ver in your hair, you won't have to ask if I still care,
Am C/G
And though I'll make mis - takes,
'cause as time turns the page,
D7/F♯ Dm/G G7
I'll nev - er break your heart.
my love won't age at all.
I swear,

C
Am
Em
by the moon and the stars in the sky,
I'll be there.
mf
F
G
C
Am
I swear,
like a sha - dow that's by your side,
Em
F
G
Dm7
I'll be there.
For
bet - ter or worse, till
G7
Dm7
To Coda
death do us part,
I'll
love you with ev - er - y beat

1.
G7
C
Am
of my heart, I swear.
mp
Em
F/G
G7
2.
G7
D.S. al Coda
of my heart. I swear,
Coda
G7
C
of my heart, I swear.
Am
Dm7
G7
C
I
swear.
mp
p

THE KEEPER OF THE STARS

Words and Music by
KAREN STALEY, DANNY MAYO and DICKEY LEE
Arranged by DAN COATES

C/E
Dm
B♭
can't be - lieve — you're in my life.
don't de - serve — a trea - sure like you.
F
Gm
Heav - en's smil - in' down — on me as I look at you to -
There — real - ly are — no words to show my grat - i -
C7sus4
C
F/A
B♭
night.
tude.
I tip my hat
mf
C
Am
B♭
to the keep - er of the stars.
He sure knew what he was

Gm
C7
F
do - in'
when he joined these two hearts.
B♭
C
I hold ev - 'ry - thing
when I hold you in my
Am
B♭
F/A
Gm
arms.
I've got all I'll ev - er need
1.
C7
B♭
F
C7
thanks to the keep- er of the stars.

2.
C7
F
thanks to the keep - er of
the stars.
C/E
Dm
It was no
ac - ci - dent,
me find - ing
mp
B♭
F
you.
Some - one had a
hand in it
Gm
C7
F
B♭/C
C7
F
long be - fore we ev - er
knew.
dim. e rit.
p

LIKE THE RAIN

Words and Music by
CLINT BLACK and HAYDEN NICHOLAS
Arranged by DAN COATES

1.
D
C
Bm7
B♭
nev - er liked the rain __ un - til I walked through it with you. __ 2. I
2.3.
D
C
Bm7
B♭
hear it, I just can't be - lieve I nev - er liked the rain. __ Like the
cresc.
Chorus:
D
F
C
G
rain, I have fall - en for you and I know just why you liked the
mf
D
F
C
G
rain al - ways call - ing for you, I'm fall - ing for you now just like __ the

1.
D
C
G/B
C
rain.
D
C
G/B
C
2.
D
F
C
G
D
rain. I have fall - en for you, I'm fall - ing for you now, just like the rain. And when the
C
D
night falls on our bet - ter days and we're look - in' to the sky for the
f

C
D
winds to take us high a - bove the plains, I
C
D
know that we'll find bet - ter ways
to look in - to the eye of the
C
G/B
storms that will be call - ing, for - ev - er we'll be fall - ing. Like the
D
F
C
G
rain, I have fall - en for you, and I know just why you like the
mf
D
F
C
G
rain al - ways call - ing for you. I'm fall - ing for you now just like the

Verse 2:
I hear it falling in the night and filling up my mind.
All the heavens' rivers come to light and I see it all unwind.
I hear it talking through the trees and on the window pane,
And when I hear it, I just can't believe I never liked the rain.
Like the rain... *(To Chorus:)*

Verse 3:
When the cloud is rolling over, thunder striking me,
It's as bright as lightning and I wonder why I couldn't see
That it's always good and when the flood is gone we still remain.
Guess I've known all along I just belong here with you falling
Like the rain... *(To Chorus:)*

MORE THAN WORDS

Lyrics and Music by
BETTENCOURT, CHERONE
Arranged by DAN COATES

Am
D7
G
Bm/F♯
eas - sy it would be to show me how you feel,
Em
Am
D7
more than words is all you have to
mf
G7
C
Cm
do to make it real. Then you would - n't have to say
G
Em7
Am
that you love me, 'cause I'd al -

D
G
G/B
read - y
know. What
would you
mp
D
Em
C
do if my heart was torn in two?
More than words
Am
D7
to show you feel
that your love for me is real.
G
G/B
D
What
would you
say if I took
mf

Em
C
those words a - way?
Then you could - n't make things new
cresc.
Am
D7
G
just by say - in' "I love you."
f
C
G/B
Am7
G/B
C
D7
mf
More than
1.
G
C
G/B
Am7
D7
words.

Verse 2:
Now that I have tried to talk to you
And make you understand,
All you have to do is close your eyes
And just reach out your hands
And touch me, hold me close, don't ever let me go.
More than words is all I ever needed you to show.
Then you wouldn't have to say
That you love me, 'cause I'd already know.

NOW AND FOREVER

Music and Lyrics by
RICHARD MARX
Arranged by DAN COATES

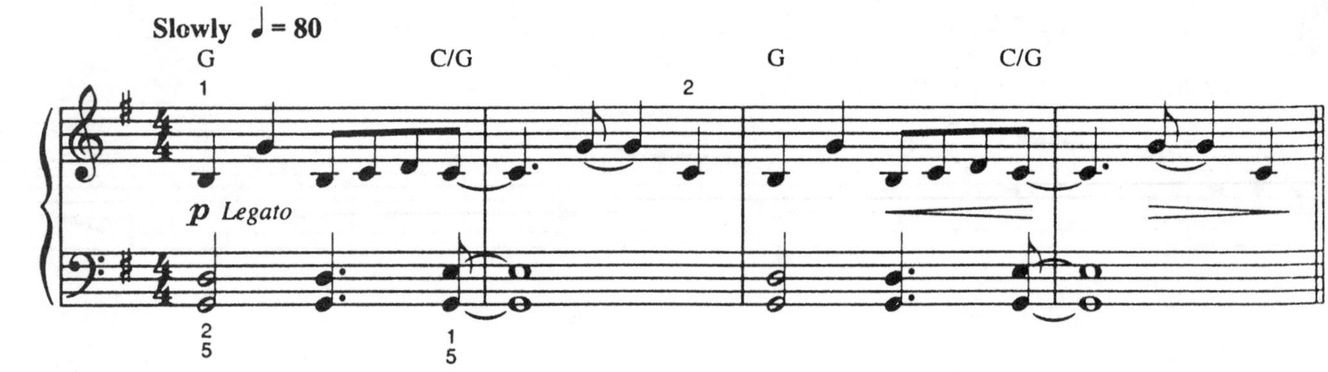

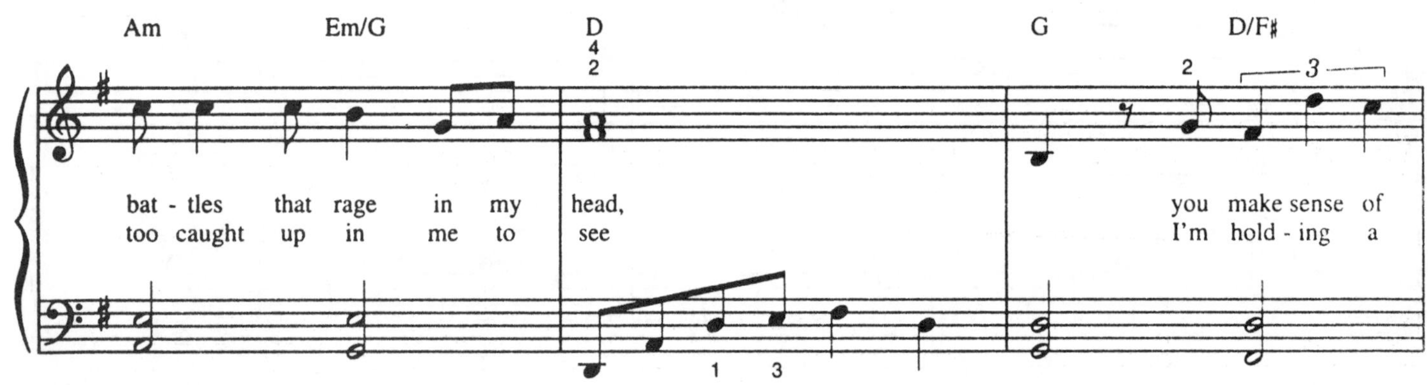

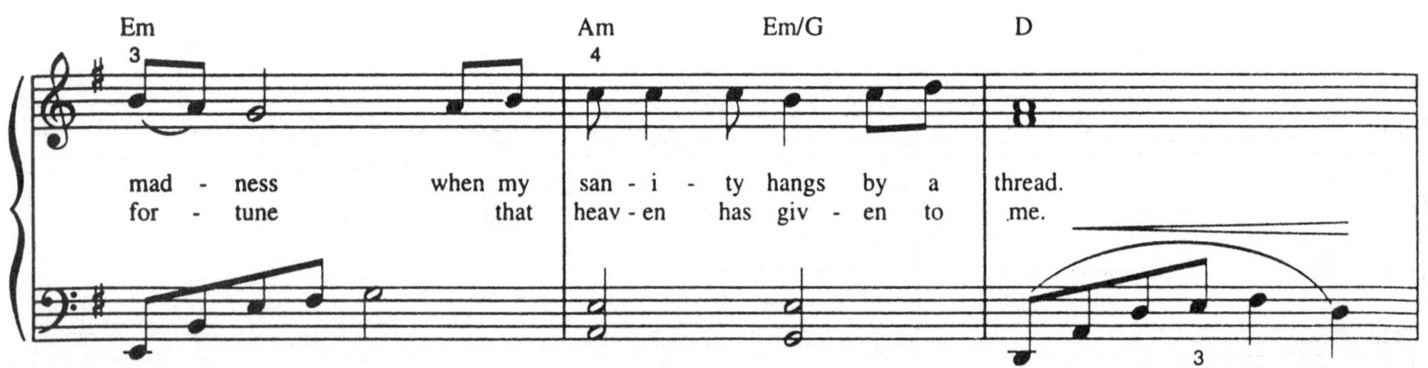

C
B7
Em
Em/D
I lose my way, but still you seem to un - der -
I'll try to show you each and ev - 'ry way I
Un - til the day the o - cean does - n't touch the
mf
A7/C♯
Am7
G/D
D7
To Coda
stand. Now and for - ev - er, I will be your
can, now and for - ev - er, I will be your
sand, now and for - ev - er, I will be your
1.
G
C/G
man.
2.
G
C/G
B7
Em
C
G
D
Now I can rest my wor - ries and al - ways be sure
mf

Em
C
G
D
Em
C
that I won't be a - lone an - y - more.
If I'd on - ly known
G
D
Am7
Cm6
D.S. 𝄋 al Coda
you were there all the time, all the time.
Coda
G
C/G
Am7
man.
Now and for - ev - er,
mp
C/D
D
C
I will be your man.
Cm
G
C/G
D/G
G
p
rit. poco a poco
pp

OPEN ARMS

Words and Music by
STEVE PERRY and
JOHNATHAN CAIN
Arranged by DAN COATES

Dm C/E F C
drift - ed a - part, and here you ___ are by my
night in - to day, I need you to
B♭ C/B♭ B♭ B♭/C C7
side. ___
stay. ___
cresc.
So now I
F Am
come ___ to you with o - pen arms, ___
mf
B♭ E♭7
noth - ing to hide, be - lieve what I say. So

F
Am
here I am with o - pen arms,
B♭
E♭7
hop - ing to see what your love means to me; o - pen
dim.
F
1.
C/E
B♭/D
arms.
mp
Dm
Am/C
B♭
2. F/E♭
B♭/D
E♭7
F
mp
rit. e dim.
p

O PERFECT LOVE

Words by
D.F. BLOMFIELD

Music by
JOSEPH BARNBY
Arranged by DAN COATES

Dm7
G7
C
C♯dim7
Dm
G7
F/C
C
whom Thou for - ev - er - more dost join in one.
G
C
E
Am
E7
Am
F♯7
O per - fect life, be Thou their full as - sur - ance
mf
B
Edim7
B
F♯7
B
of ten - der char - i - ty and stead - fast faith; of
Fdim
E7
A
E7
C+
C
pa - tient hope and qui - et, brave en - dur - ance, with
mp

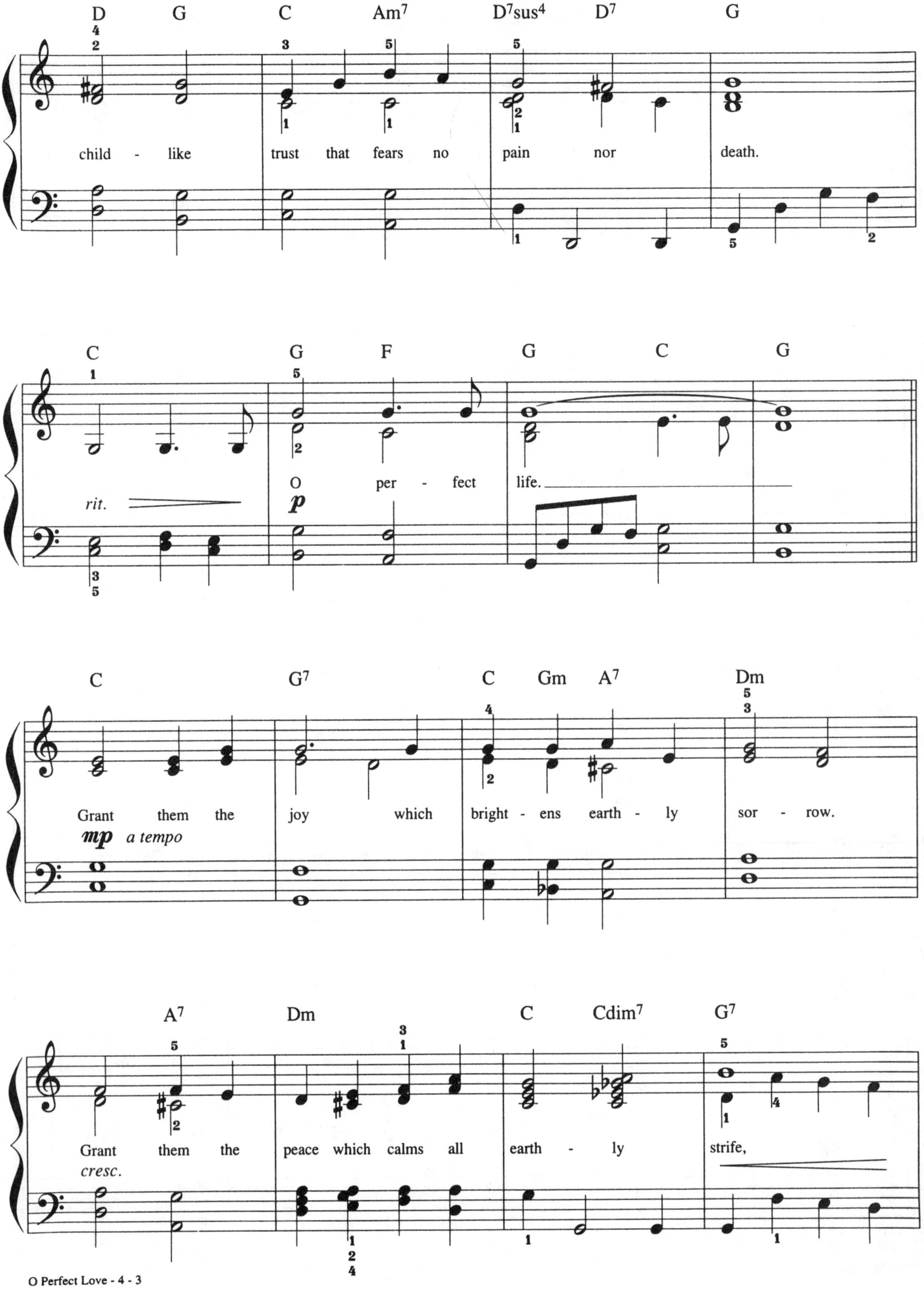

D G C Am7 D7sus4 D7 G

child - like trust that fears no pain nor death.

C G F G C G

O per - fect life.

rit. *p*

C G7 C Gm A7 Dm

Grant them the joy which bright - ens earth - ly sor - row.

mp *a tempo*

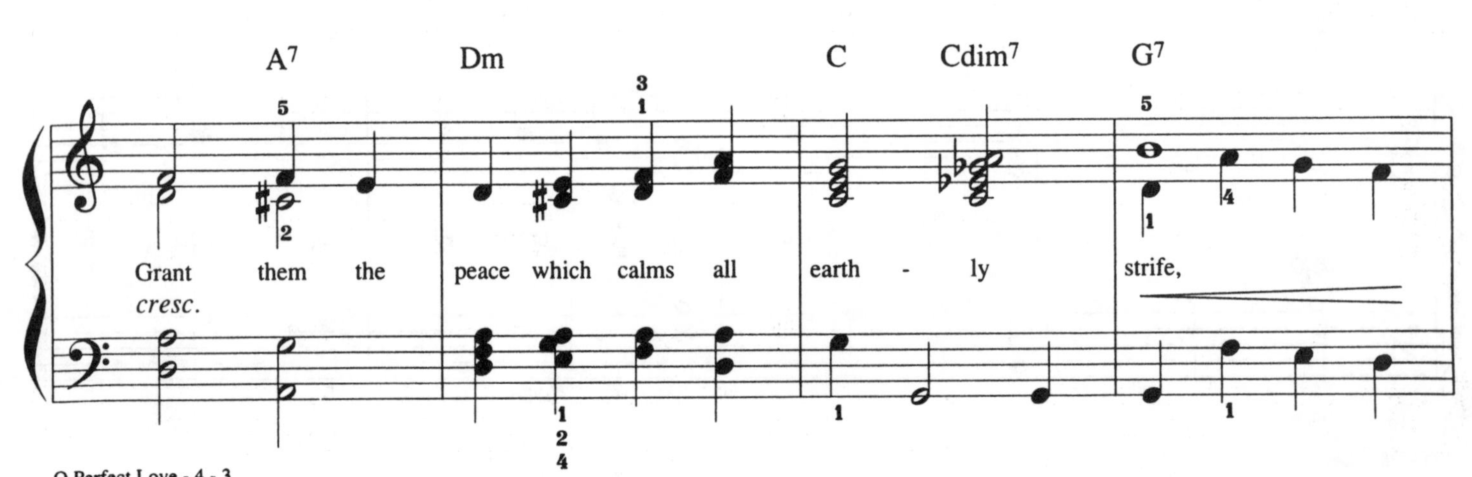

Am7
D7
G
C
and to life's day the glo - rious un - known mor - row that
F
C
G♯dim
Am
C♯dim7
Dm
G7
C
G7
dawns up - on e - ter - nal love and life.
mf
C
Dm7
C
F
A7
Dm
F
And to life's day the glo - rious un - known
cresc.
G
C
F
C
G7
mor - row that dawns up - on e - ter - nal love and
f
ff
rit.
C
G7
C
F
C
G
Csus4
C
life. A - men, A - men.
mp
pp
f
dim.

PACHELBEL CANON IN D

JOHANN PACHELBEL
(1653-1706)
Arranged by DAN COATES

D
A
Bm
F♯m
mf
G
D
G
A
cresc.
D
A
Bm
F♯m
f
G
D
G
A

D
A
Bm
F♯m
ff
G
D
G
A
f
dim.
D
A
Bm
F♯m
mf
G
D
G
A

D
A
Bm
F#m
G
D
f
decresc.
G
A
D
A
Bm
F#m
mp
G
D
G
A
D
A
p
Bm
F#m
G
D
G
A
A7
D
rit. e dim.
pp

From the Twentieth Century-Fox Motion Picture "THE ROSE"

THE ROSE

Words and Music by
AMANDA McBROOM
Arranged by DAN COATES

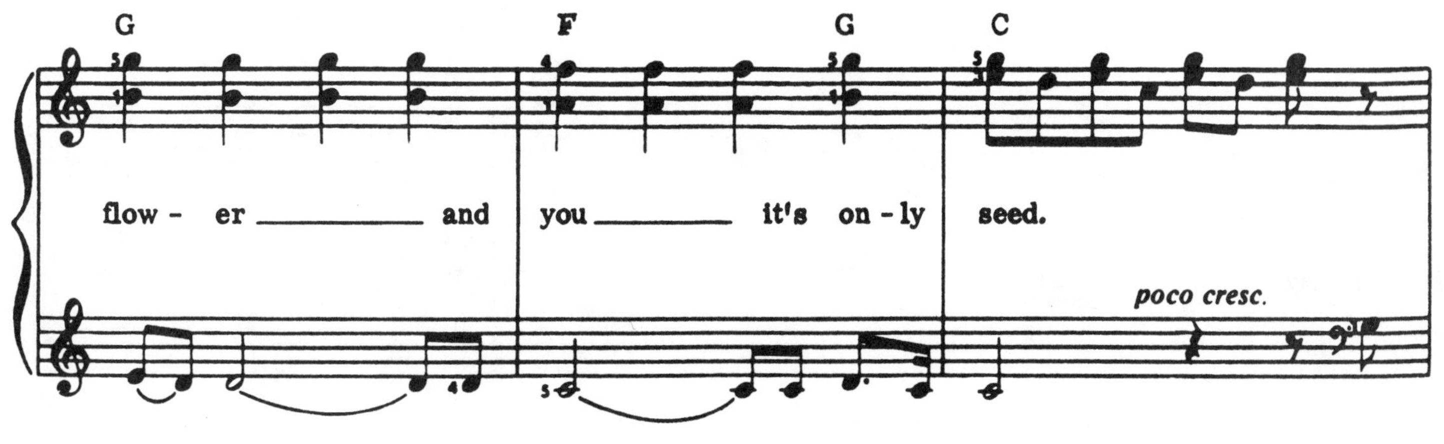
G
F
G
C
flow - er and
you it's on - ly
seed.
poco cresc.

C
It's the
heart a - fraid of
night has been too
mf

G
F
G
C
break - ing that
lone - ly and the
nev-er learns to
road has been too
dance. It's the
long, and you

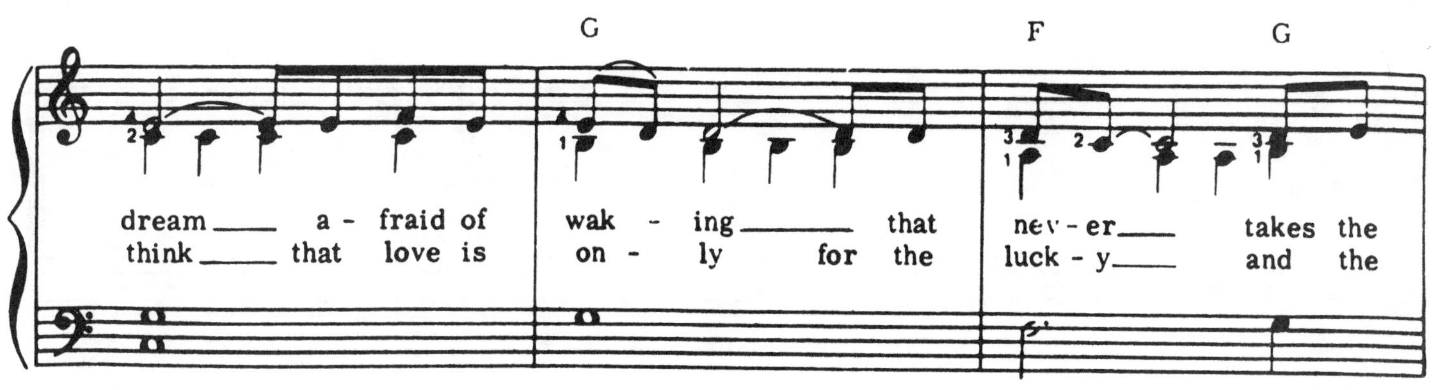
G
F
G
dream a - fraid of
think that love is
wak - ing that
on - ly for the
nev - er takes the
luck - y and the

C Em Am C/G
chance. It's the one who won't be tak - en who
strong, just re - mem - ber in the win - ter far be -
F G7 C
can not seem to give, and the soul a - fraid of
neath the bit - ter snows lies the seed that with the
G
dy - ing that
sun's love in the
1.
F G
nev - er learns to
C
live. When the
cresc.
2.
F G
spring be - comes the
rit.
C
rose.
a tempo
rit. e dim.
p

YOU NEEDED ME

Words and Music by
RANDY GOODRUM
Arranged by DAN COATES

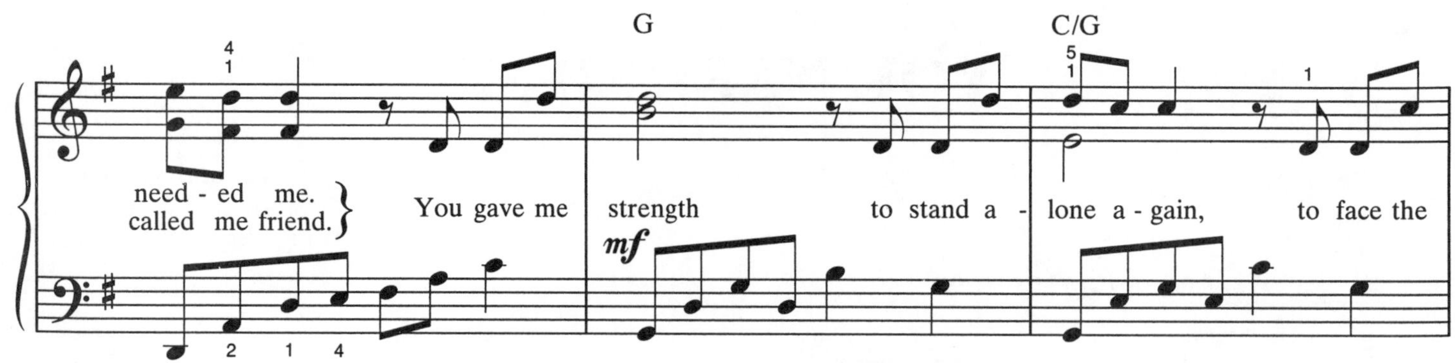
G
C/G
need - ed me.
called me friend.
You gave me
strength
to stand a - lone a - gain,
to face the
mf

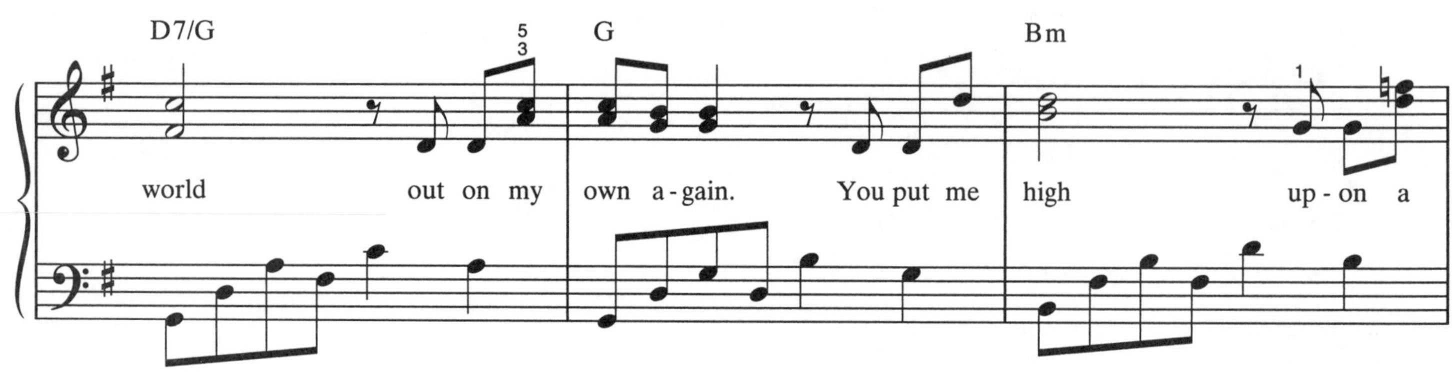
D7/G
G
Bm
world
out on my
own a - gain.
You put me
high
up - on a

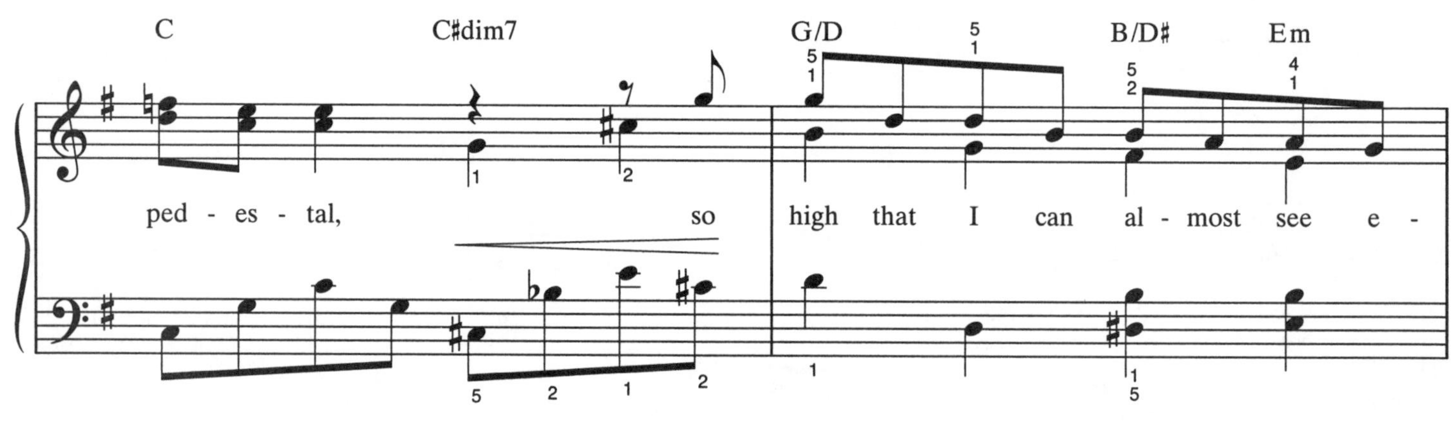
C
C♯dim7
G/D
B/D♯
Em
ped - es - tal,
so
high that I can al - most see e -

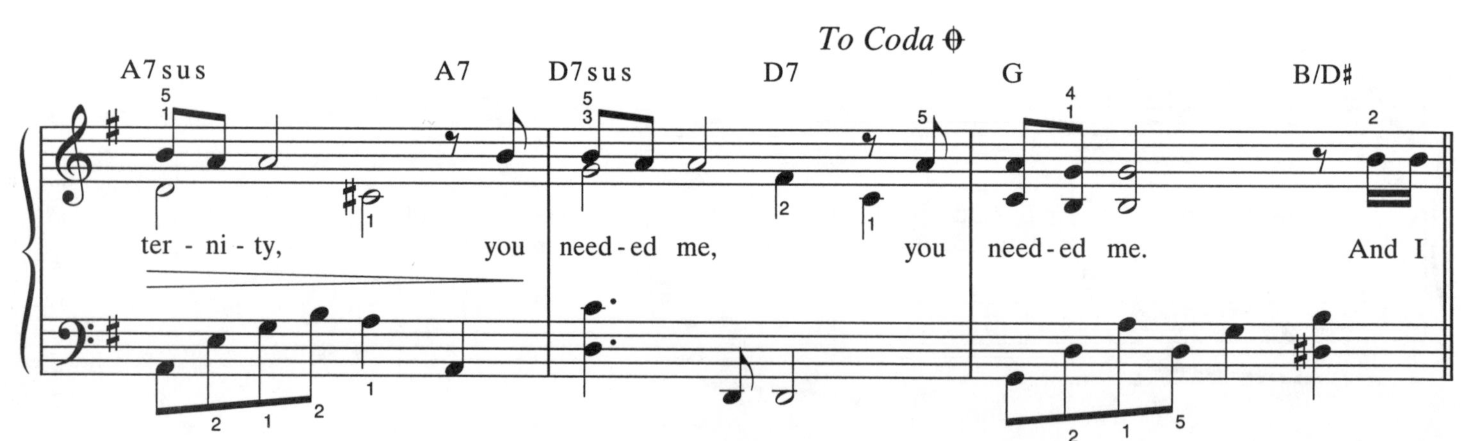
To Coda
A7sus
A7
D7sus
D7
G
B/D♯
ter - ni - ty,
you
need - ed me,
you
need - ed me.
And I

Em G/D C G/B Am7 C/D
can't be-lieve it's you, I can't be - lieve it's true. I need-ed you and you were
G B7 Em G/D
there___ and I'll nev - er leave. Why should I leave? I'd
C G/B A7sus A7 D7sus
be a fool 'cause I've fi-n'lly found some-one who real-ly cares.
dim.
D.S. al Coda
Coda
C/D D7 G E7 A7 D7
2. You held my
need-ed me. You need-ed me, you
G E7 Am7 D7 G
need-ed me.
rit.

Theme from LOVE AFFAIR

Music by
ENNIO MORRICONE
Arranged by DAN COATES

Theme from Love Affair - 2 - 1

B♭
B♭m
F/A
A♭dim
Gm7
diminuendo
mp
F/C
B♭/C
F
B♭/F
poco rit.
p
F
Gm7
F/A
mf
B♭maj7
B♭maj7/C
Gm7
G♯dim7
Am7
Dm7
cresc.
f
mf
Gm7
C7
F(add2)
8va
rit. e dim.
p
pp

TONIGHT I CELEBRATE MY LOVE

Words and Music by
MICHAEL MASSER and GERRY GOFFIN
Arranged by DAN COATES

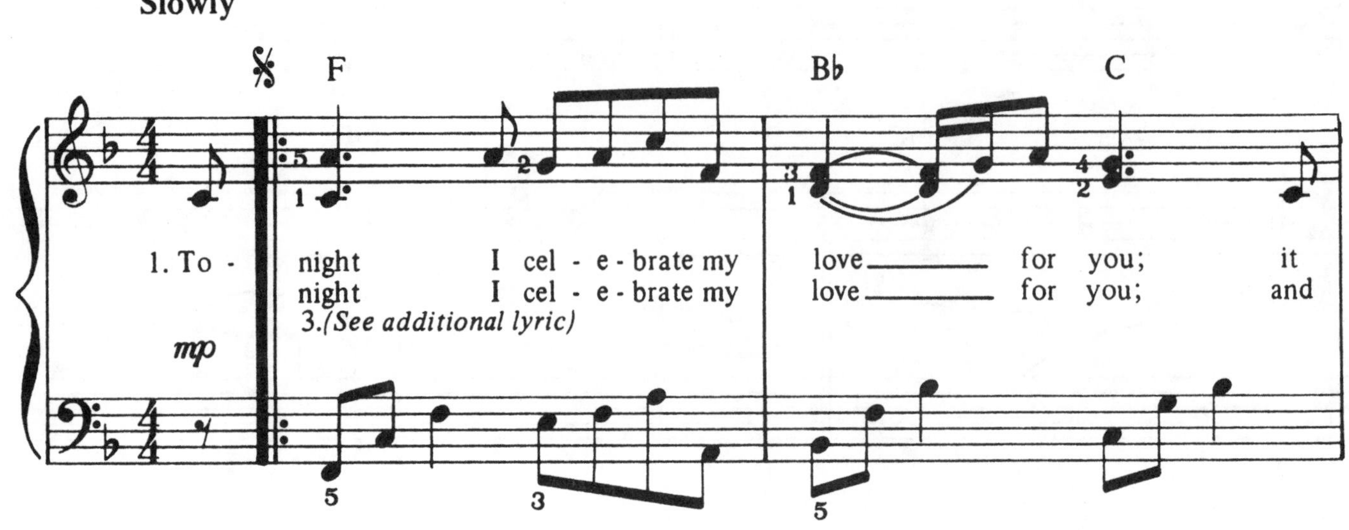
Slowly
F
Bb
C
1. To -
night I cel - e - brate my love for you; it
night I cel - e - brate my love for you; and
3.(See additional lyric)
mp

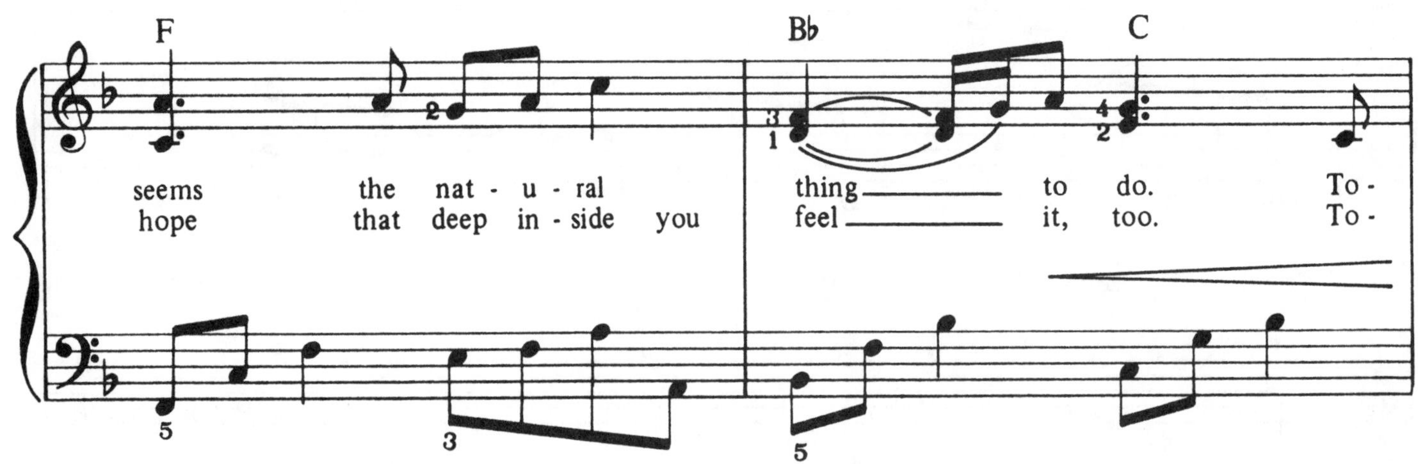
F
Bb
C
seems the nat - u - ral thing to do. To -
hope that deep in - side you feel it, too. To -

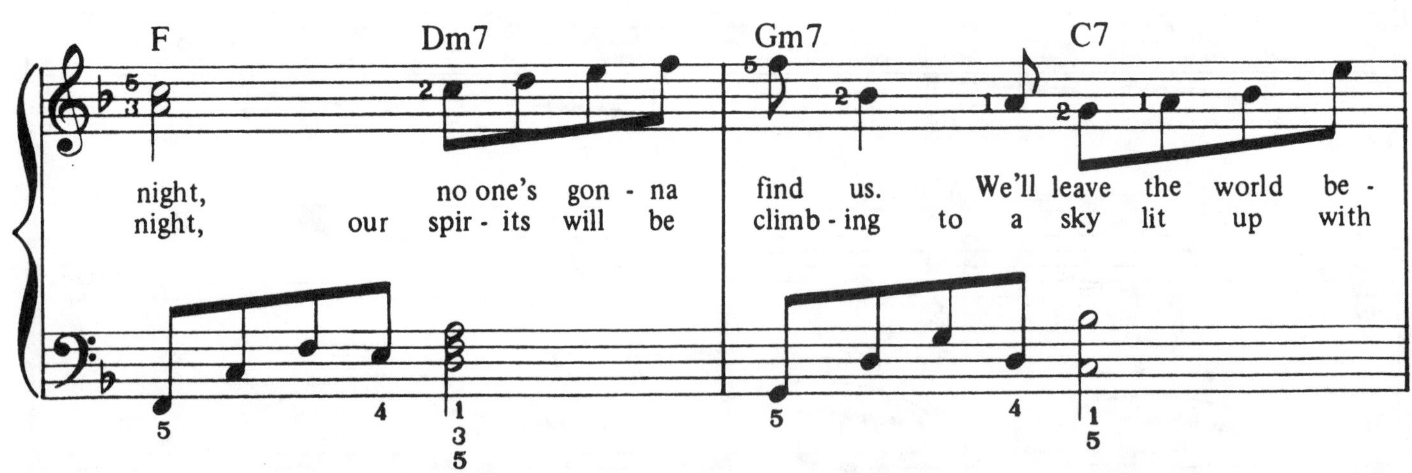
F
Dm7
Gm7
C7
night, no one's gon - na find us. We'll leave the world be -
night, our spir - its will be climb - ing to a sky lit up with

Am7
Dm7
3
1.
Gm7
Bb/C
hind us,
dia - monds,
when I make
when I make
love to you.
2. To -
mp
2. Bbmaj7
Bb/C
F
love to you
to -
night.
Bb/F
To next strain
3.Bbmaj7
Bb/C
To -
love to you.
To -
(cresc.)
Bbmaj7
Am7
Eb/F
F7
night,
I cel - e - brate my
love for you,
and the
f
Bbmaj7
Am7
Eb/F
F7
mid - night sun
is gon - na come
shin - ing through.
To -

Verse 3:

Tonight I celebrate my love for you
And soon this old world will seem brand new.
Tonight we will both discover
How friends turn into lovers.
When I make love to you.

I TURN TO YOU

Words and Music by
DIANE WARREN
Arranged by DAN COATES

F
C/E
— los - ing ground, when my
— an - y - thing, 'cause your
A♭maj7
Gm7
world is go - ing cra - zy, you can turn it all a - round.
love is so a - maz - ing, 'cause your love in - spi - res me.
A7
Dm
And when I'm down, you're there, push - ing me to the top.
And when I need a friend, you're al - ways on my side,
Gm7
C7sus
You're al - ways there giv - ing me all you've got.
giv - ing me faith, tak - ing me through the night.
For a shield

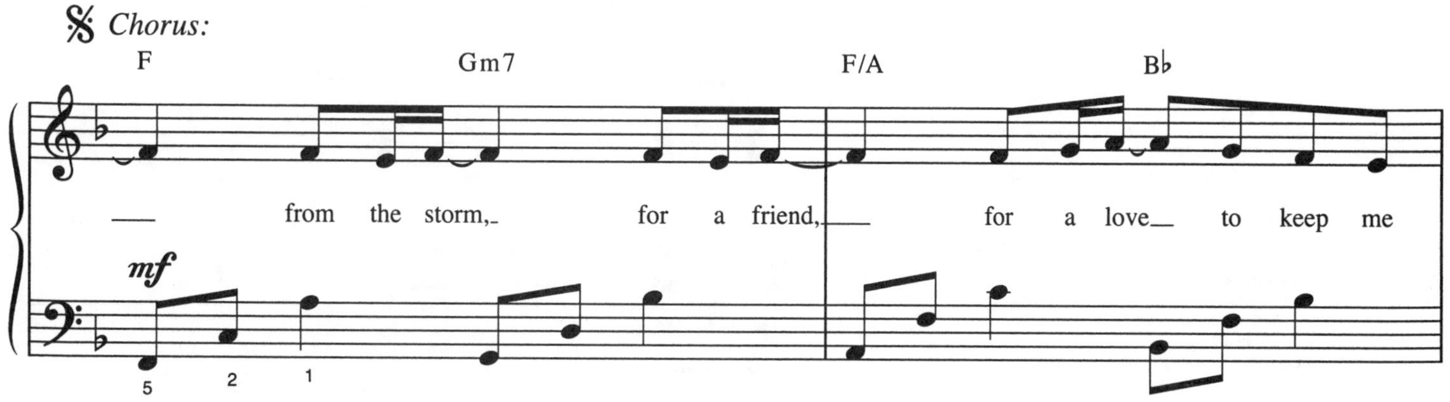
Chorus:
F
Gm7
F/A
B♭
from the storm, for a friend, for a love to keep me
mf

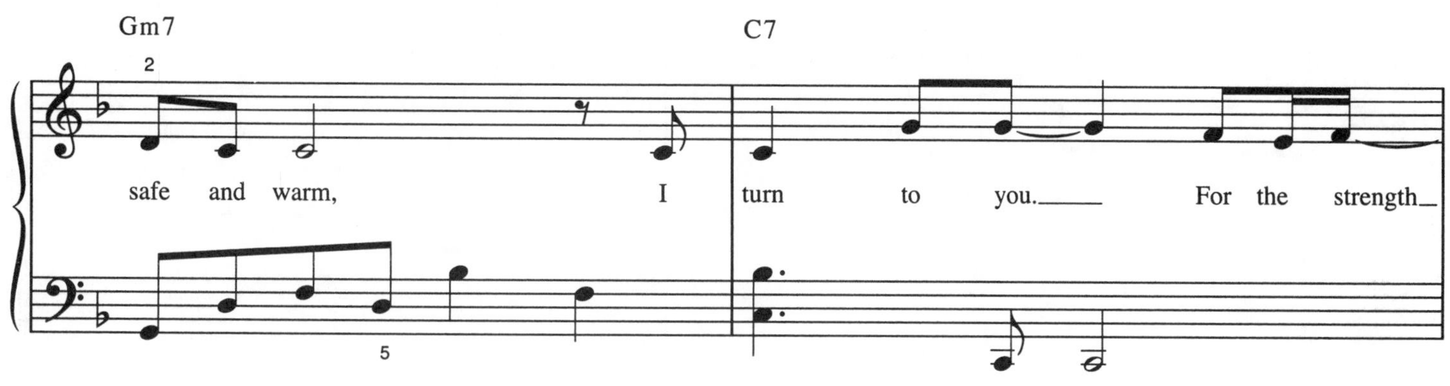
Gm7
C7
safe and warm, I turn to you. For the strength

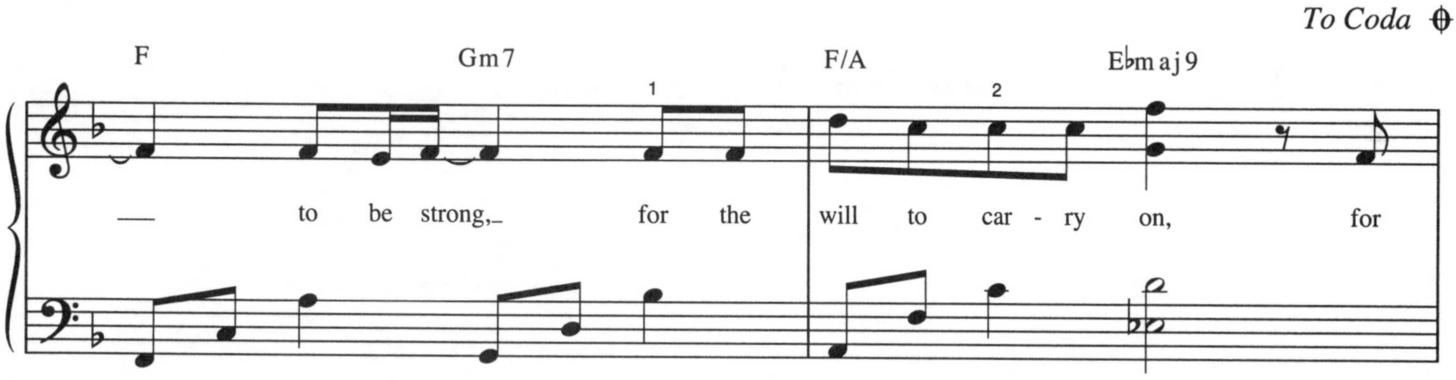
To Coda
F
Gm7
F/A
E♭maj9
to be strong, for the will to car - ry on, for

1.
Gm7
D♭/E♭
C7sus
ev - 'ry - thing you do, for ev - 'ry - thing that's true, I turn to

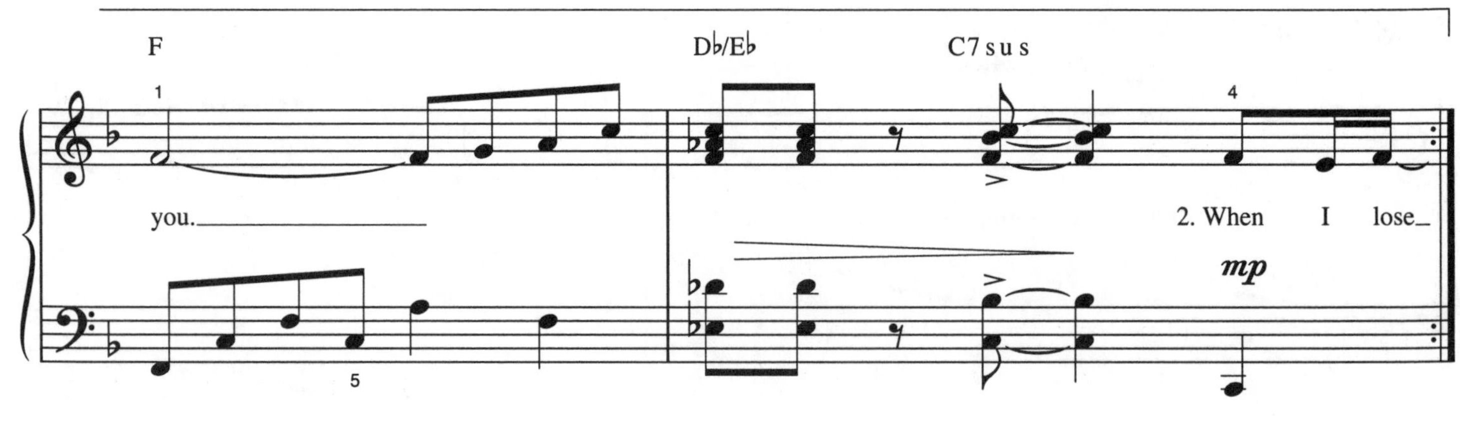
F
Db/Eb
C7sus
you.
2. When I lose
mp

2.
Gm7
C7sus
F
ev - 'ry - thing you do, I turn to
you.

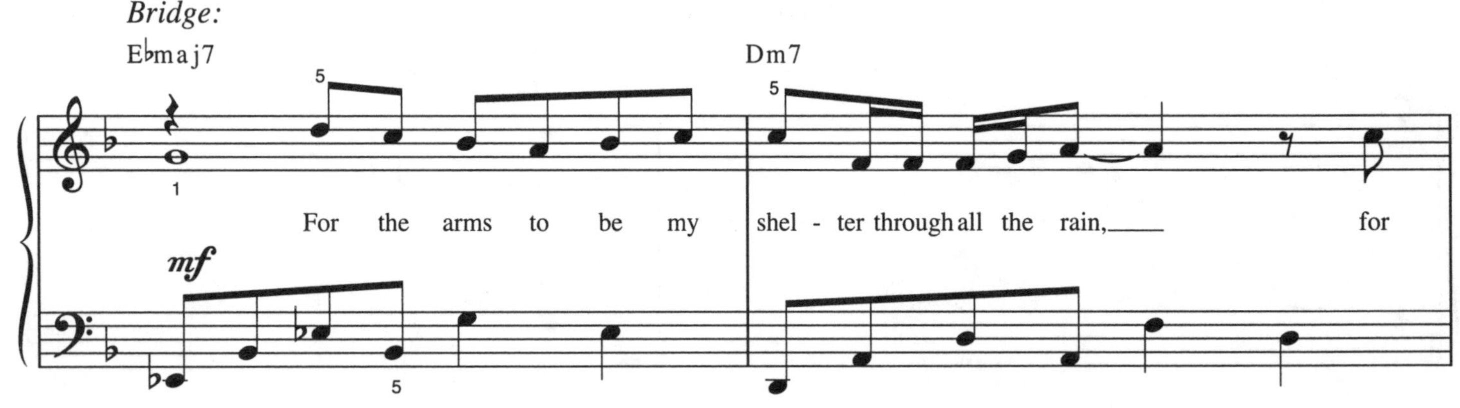
Bridge:
Ebmaj7
Dm7
For the arms to be my
shel - ter through all the rain,
for
mf

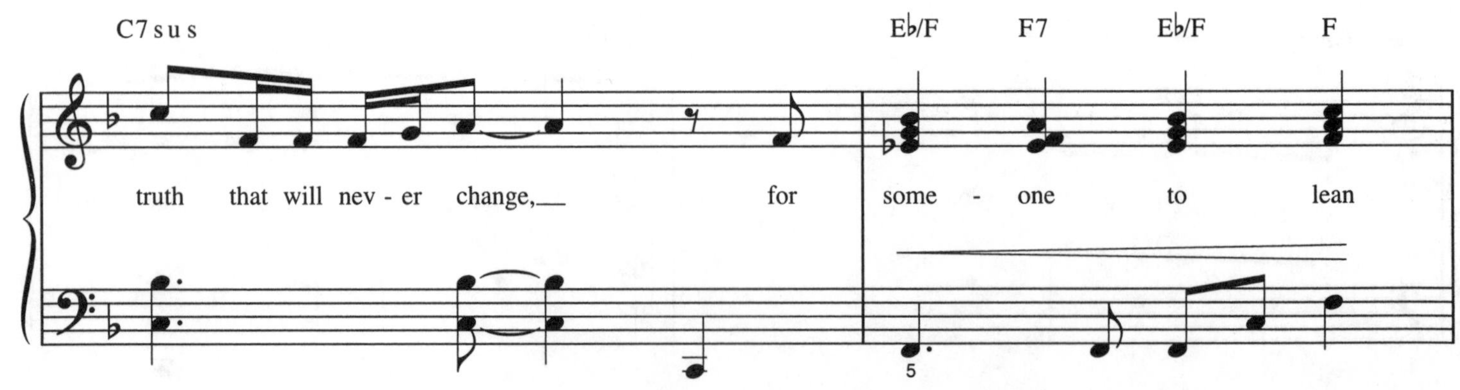
C7sus
Eb/F
F7
Eb/F
F
truth that will nev - er change,
for
some - one to lean

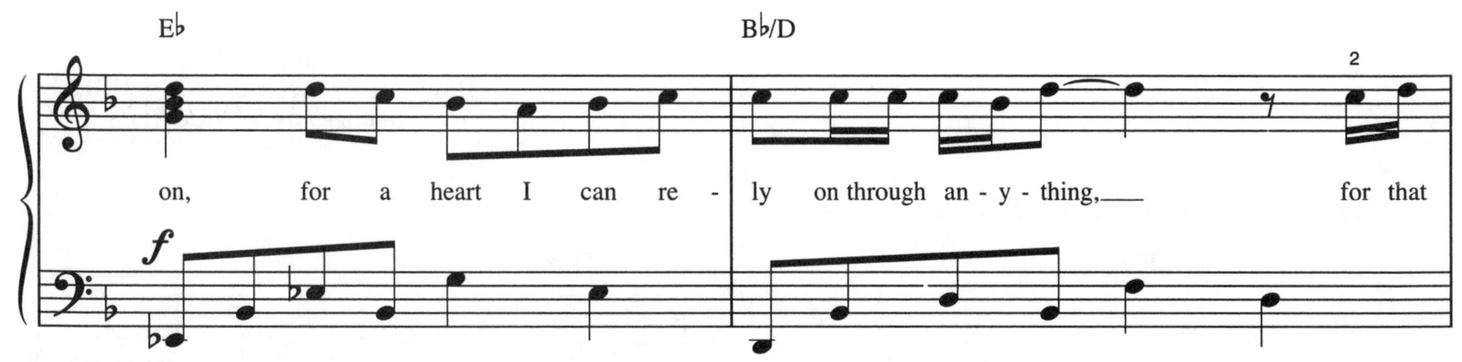
E♭
B♭/D
on, for a heart I can re - ly on through an - y - thing,__ for that
f

Gm7/C
C7
D.S. 𝄋 al Coda
one who__ I can run to. For a shield__
mf

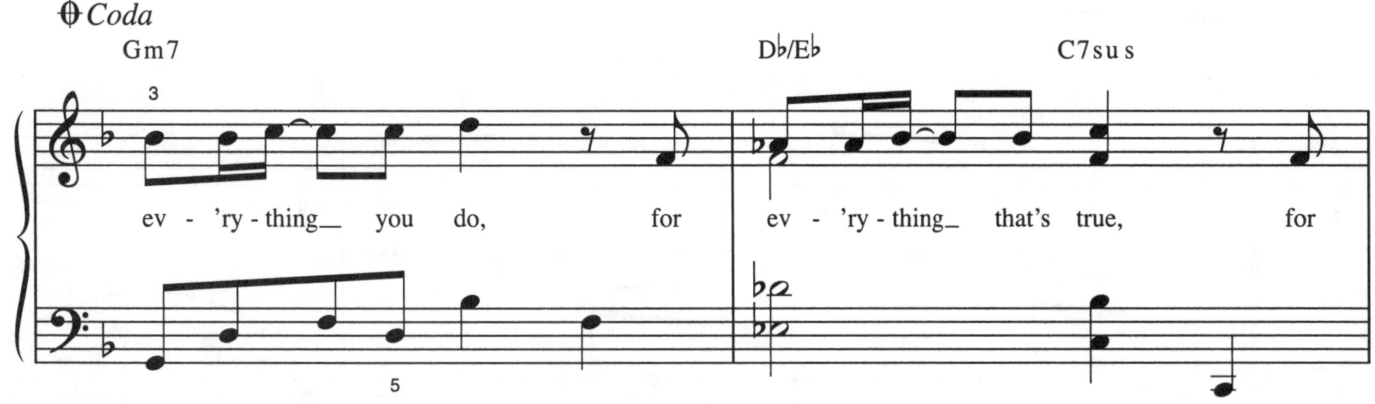
Coda
Gm7
D♭/E♭
C7sus
ev - 'ry - thing_ you do, for ev - 'ry - thing_ that's true, for

Gm7
D♭/E♭
C7sus
F
ev - 'ry - thing_ you do, for ev - 'ry-thing__that's true, I turn to you.
molto rit.
mp

VALENTINE

Composed by
JIM BRICKMAN and JACK KUGELL
Arranged by DAN COATES

B♭
C7
F/A
in - side, I'd
still feel for you. And
e - ven if the sun
mf
B♭
C
Am7
F/A
B♭
C
re - fused to shine,
e - ven if ro - mance
ran out of rhyme,
Gm7
A7sus4
A7
Dm
F/C
you would
still have my heart un -
til the end of time.
Bm7(♭5)
F/C
B♭/C
To Coda
C
You're
'Cause
all I need, my
all I need is
love,
you,
my Val - en -

1.
F
Dm
B♭
tine.
mp
B♭/C
2.
F
Dm
tine.
mp
B♭
B♭/D
C/E
F
D.S. 𝄋 al Coda
Dm
B♭
F/C
C7
cresc.
And

Verse 2:
All of my life,
I have been waiting for all you give to me.
You've opened my eyes
And shown me how to love unselfishly.
I've dreamed of this a thousand times before,
But in my dreams I couldn't love you more.
I will give you my heart until the end of time.
You're all I need, my love,
My Valentine.

A VERY PRECIOUS LOVE

Words by
PAUL FRANCIS WEBSTER

Music by
SAMMY FAIN
Arranged by DAN COATES

Gm7
C7
F
Lan - terns of gold,
mf
Em7(♭5)
A7
Dm
G7
lan - terns of blue,
twin - kle in the
C
A7
Dm7
G7
Gm7/C
C7
shad - ows while I
dance with
you.
An
F
ech - o in the wind
a - cross the sum - mer lake
mp

Am7(♭5)
D7
is
say - ing you should know that
cresc.
lan - terns lose their glow and
Gm
hearts can break.
So
Bm7
E7
hold me close, my
mf
Am7
F/A
Am7
D7
Gm7
Gm7(♭5)
dar - ling, then
kiss me ten - der -
ly. And
F/C
Gm7/C
C7(♭9)
give your pre - cious love, your
ver - y pre - cious love to
1. F
me.
mp
Gm7
C7
A
2. F
me.
rit.
p

WEDDING SONG
(There Is Love)

Arranged by DAN COATES

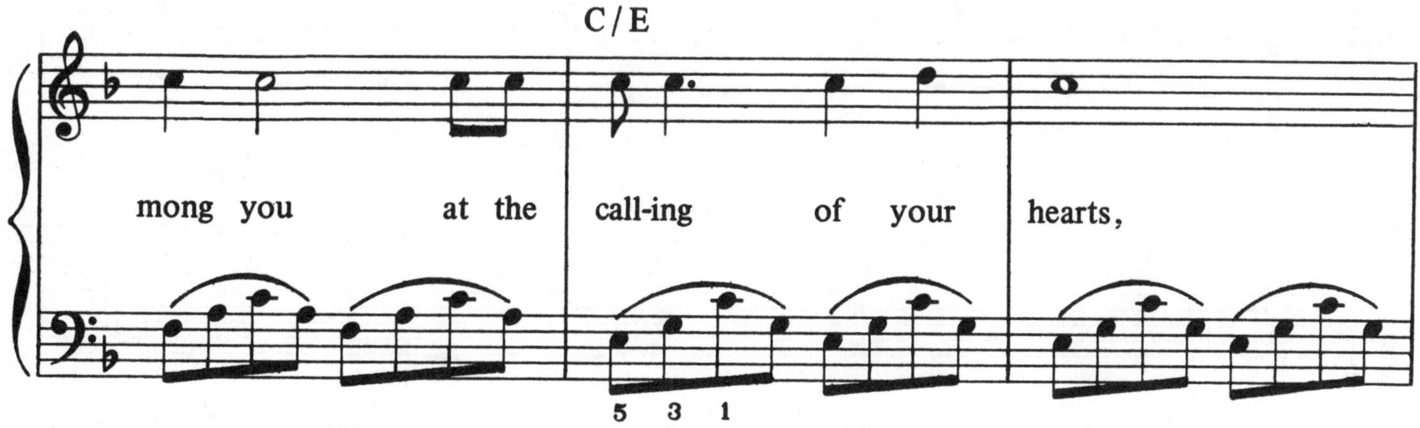

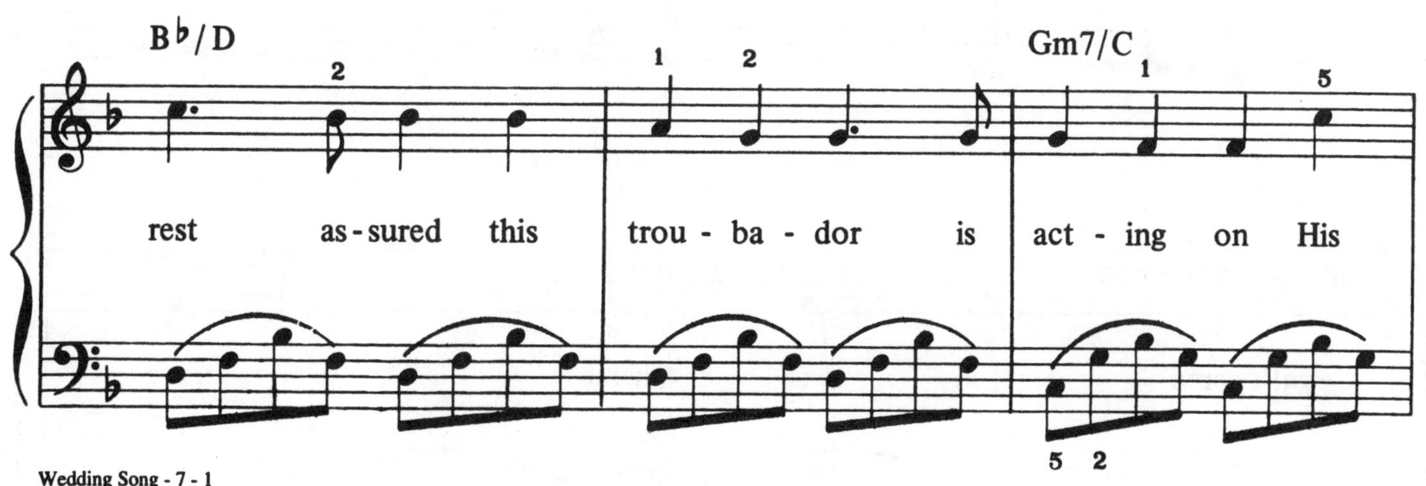

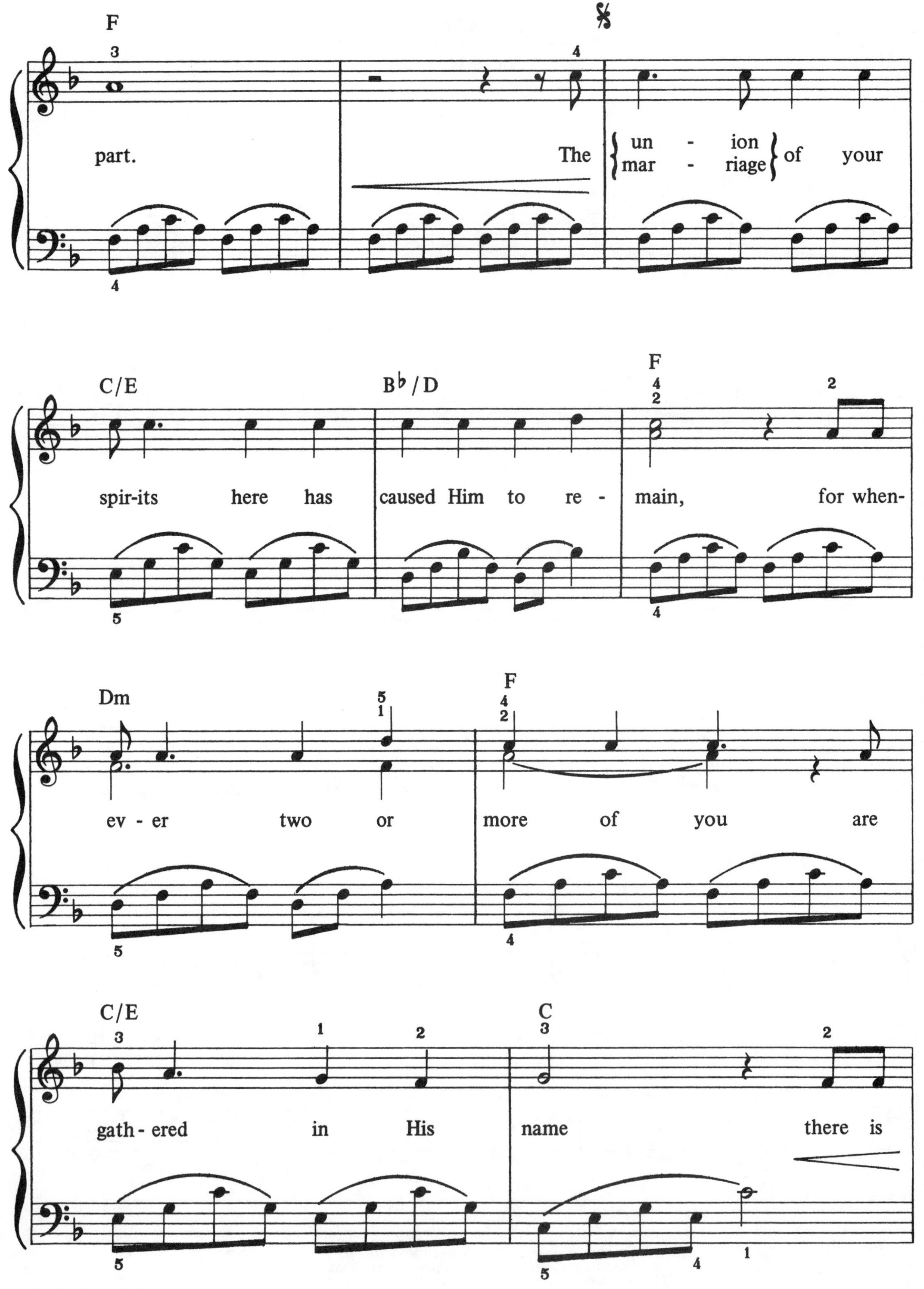
F
3
4
part.
The
un - ion
mar - riage
of your
4
C/E
B♭/D
F
4
2
2
spir-its here has
caused Him to re -
main, for when-
5
4
Dm
5
1
F
4
2
ev - er two or
more of you are
5
4
C/E
3
1
2
C
3
2
gath - ered in His
name there is
5
5
4
1

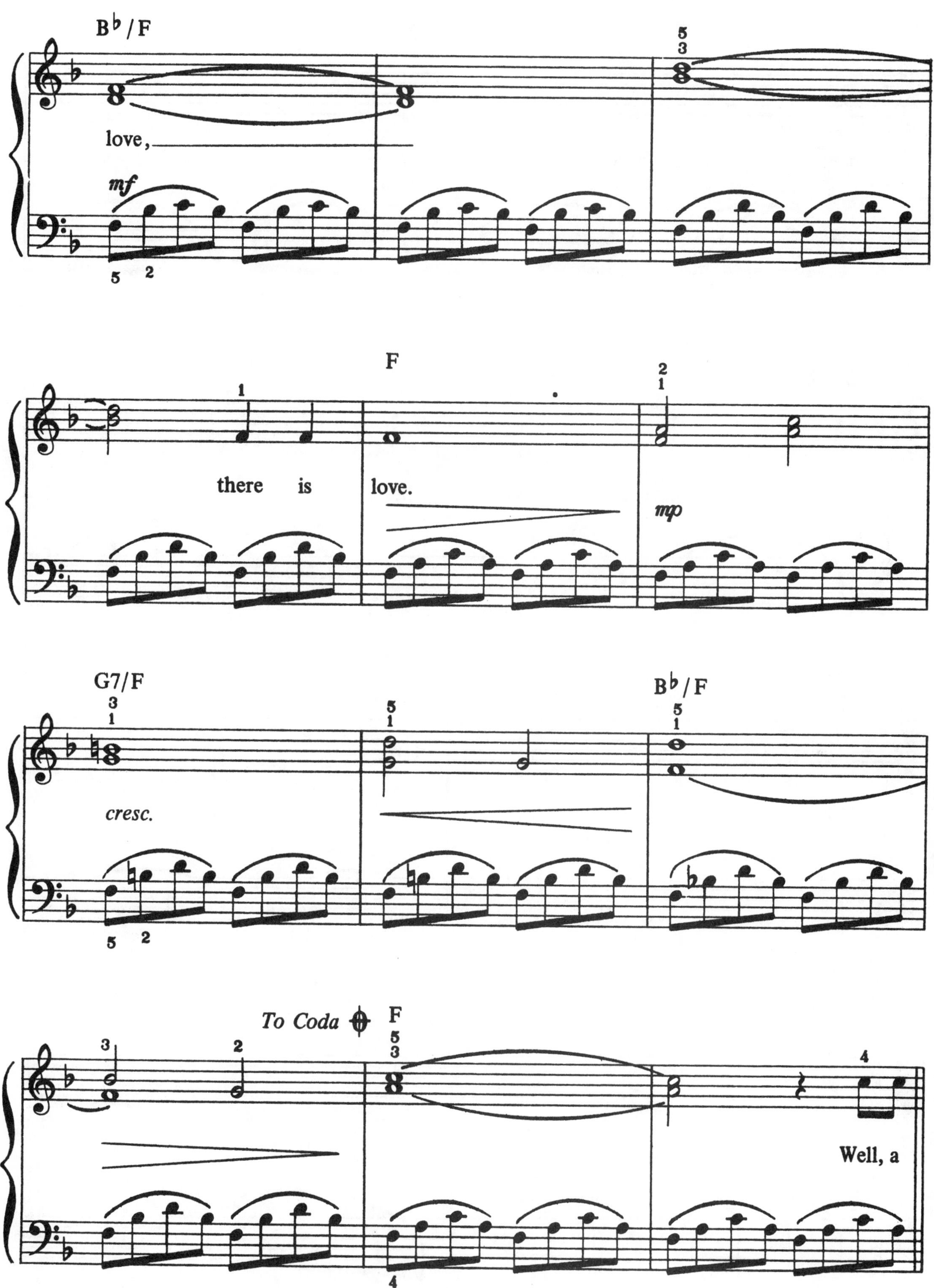
B♭/F
love,
mf
there is
love.
F
mp
G7/F
cresc.
B♭/F
To Coda
F
Well, a

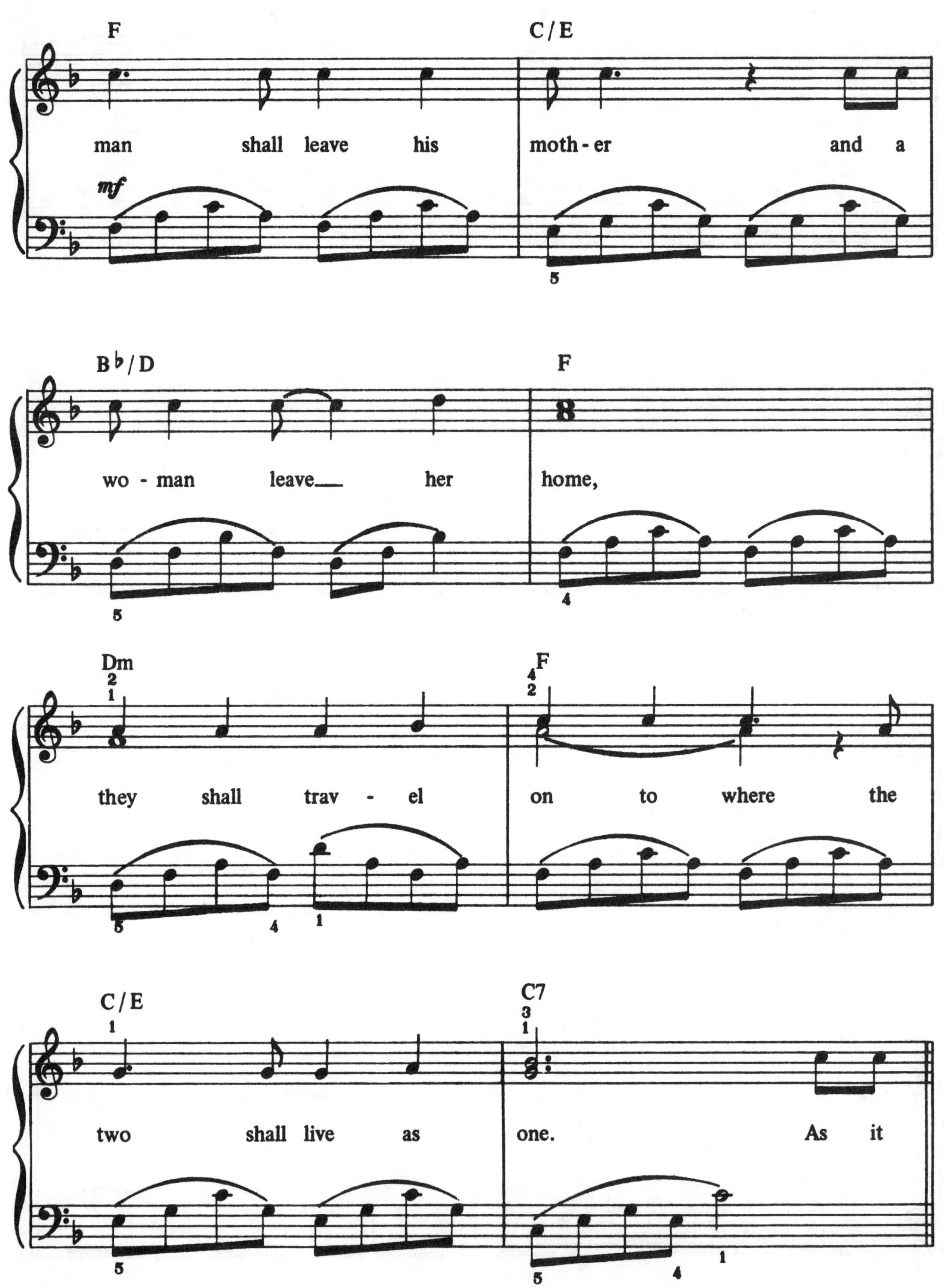
F
C/E
man shall leave his moth - er and a
mf
B♭/D
F
wo - man leave her home,
Dm
F
they shall trav - el on to where the
C/E
C7
two shall live as one. As it

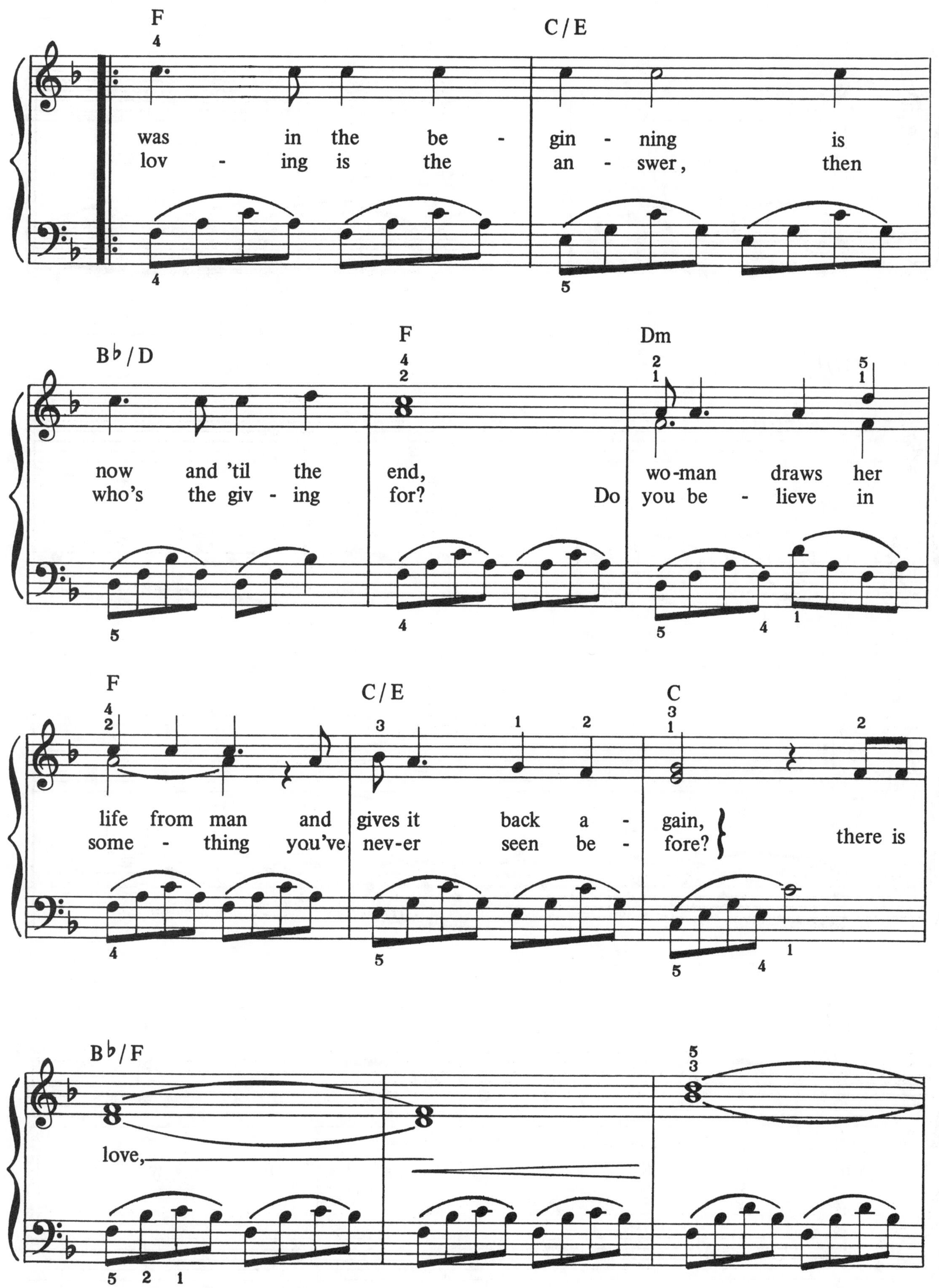
F
C/E
was in the be - gin - ning is
lov - ing is the an - swer, then
B♭/D
F
Dm
now and 'til the end, wo-man draws her
who's the giv - ing for? Do you be - lieve in
F
C/E
C
life from man and gives it back a - gain,
some - thing you've nev-er seen be - fore?
there is
B♭/F
love,

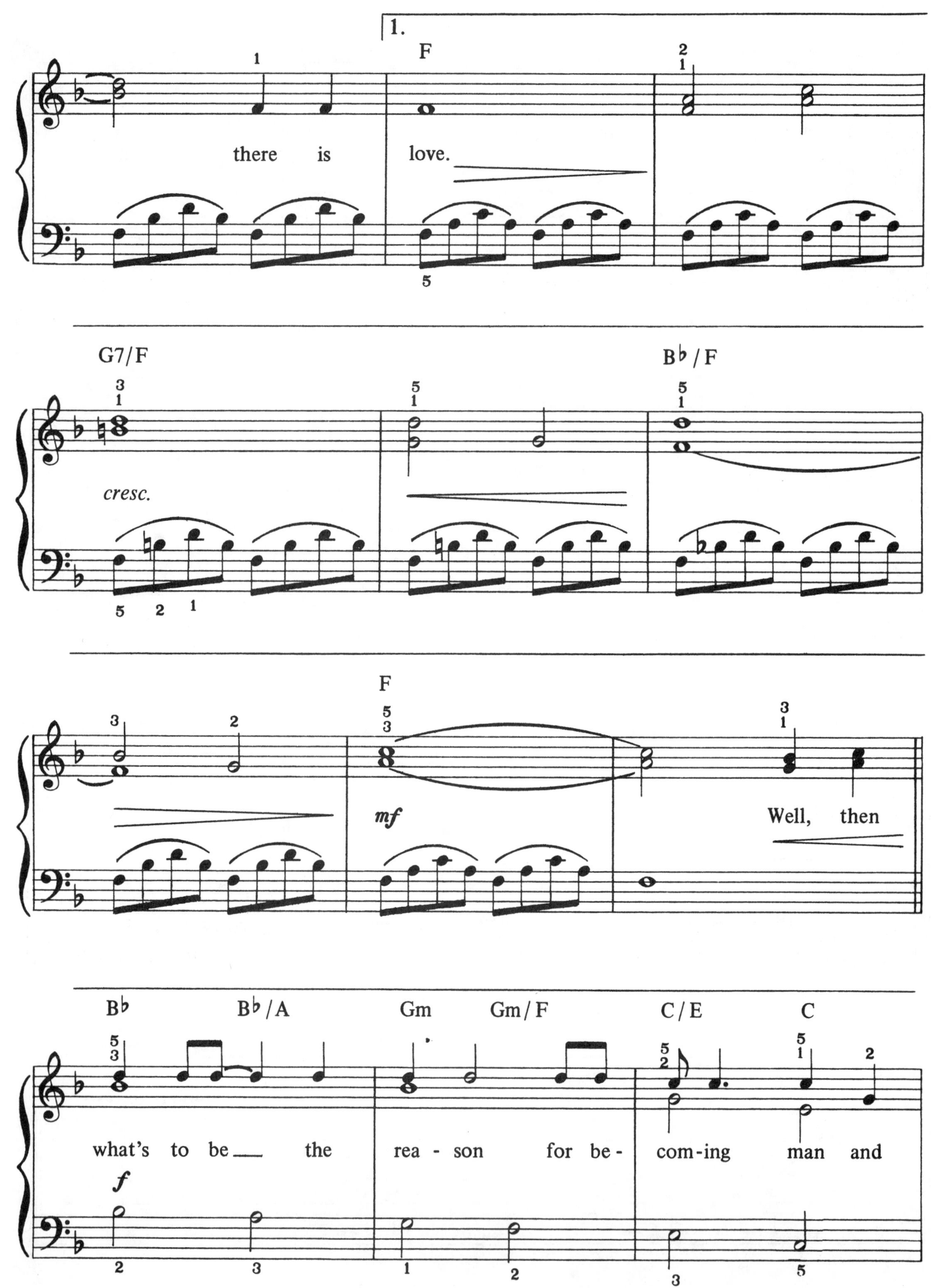
1.
F
there is
love.
G7/F
cresc.
B♭/F
F
mf
Well, then
B♭
B♭/A
Gm
Gm/F
C/E
C
what's to be the
rea - son
for be -
com-ing
man and
f

F
Bb
Bb/A
Gm
Gm/F
wife? Is it love that brings you here, or
C/E
C
F
2.
F
love that brings you life? For if love.
D. S. al Coda
dim.
Oh, the
CODA
F
p rit.
pp

WEDDING MARCH

by
FELIX MENDELSSOHN
Arranged by DAN COATES

2.
mf
f
ff
rall.
f

WHEN A MAN LOVES A WOMAN

Words and Music by
CALVIN LEWIS and ANDREW WRIGHT
Arranged by DAN COATES

Moderately slow (♩. = 60 M.M.
F
C/E
Dm
F/C
p
cresc. (poco a poco)
B♭
B♭/C
C7
F
C7
When a
F
C/E
Dm7
man loves a woman, can't keep his
man loves a woman, spend his
mf
F/C
B♭
C
B♭/C
mind on noth- in' else. He'd trade the world for the good thing he's
ver - y last dime try - ing to hold on to what he

F
Bb/C
F
C/E
found.
needs.
If she is
He'd give up
bad, he can't
all his
see it.
com - forts
Dm7
F/C
To Coda
Bb
She can
and sleep
do no wrong.
out in the rain,
Turn his back on his
if she said that's the
1.
Bb/C
F
Bb/C
best friend if he
puts her down.
When a
2.
C7
F
F7
way it ought to
be.
cresc.

Bb
F
F7
When a man loves a woman,
I give you ev-'ry-thing I've got.
C/E
Dm7
Try-ing to hold on to your pre-cious love.
G7
Bb/C
C7
D.S. al Coda
Ba-by, ba-by, please don't treat me bad.
When a

Additional Lyrics

When a man loves a woman,
Deep down in his soul,
She can bring him such misery.
If she is playing him for a fool,
He's the last one to know.
Loving eyes can never see.

From the Original Motion Picture Soundtrack "BEACHES"

THE WIND BENEATH MY WINGS

Words and Music by
LARRY HENLEY and JEFF SILBAR
Arranged by DAN COATES

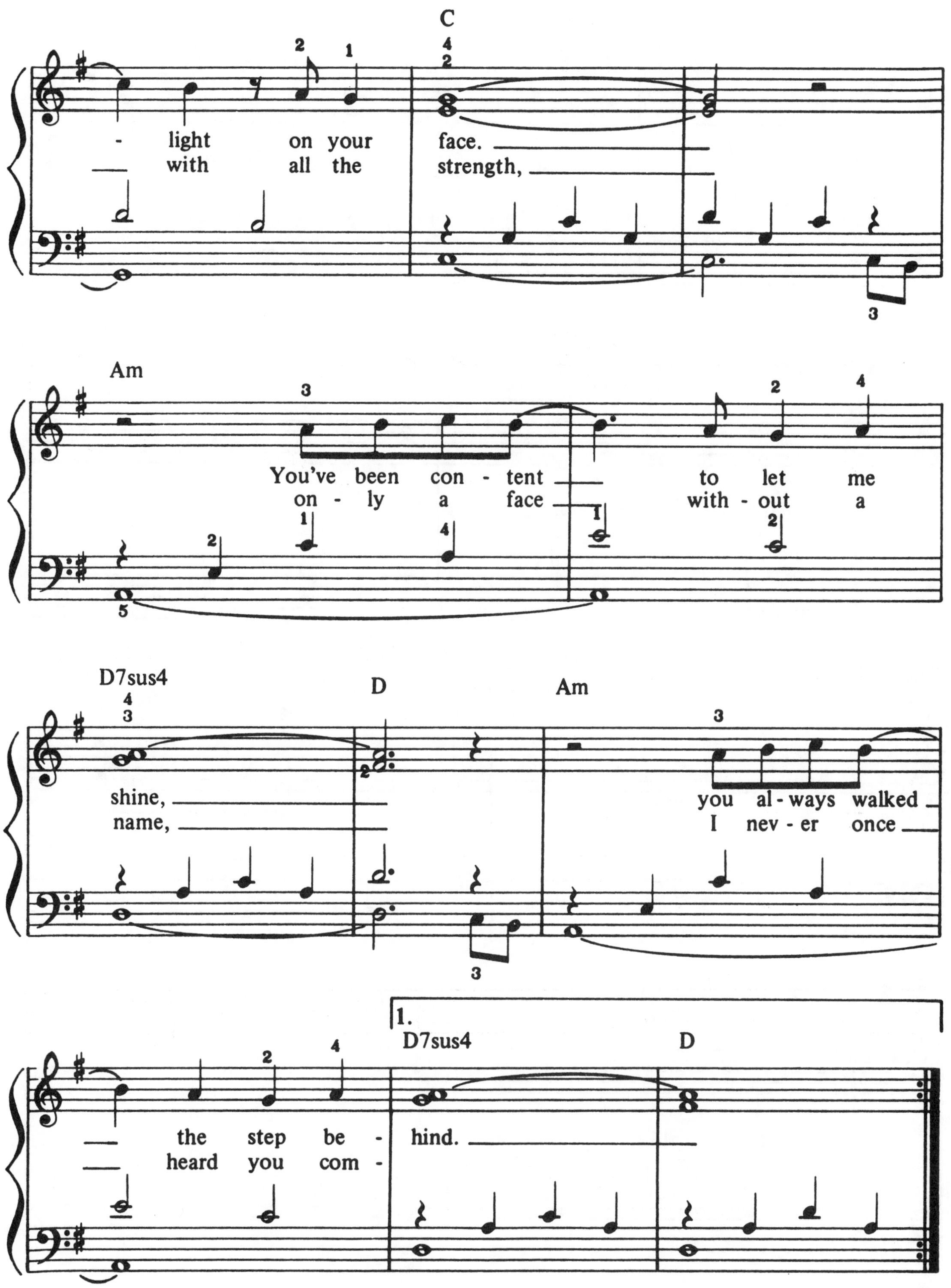
C
light on your face.
with all the strength,
Am
You've been con - tent to let me
on - ly a face with - out a
D7sus4
D
Am
shine,
name,
you al - ways walked
I nev - er once
the step be - hind.
heard you com -
1.
D7sus4
D

2.3.
D
B / D♯
Em
plain.
cresc.
mf
Did you ev - er know
C
G
that you're my
he - ro,
D / F♯
Em
and ev - 'ry - thing
C
G
I'd like to
be?

D/F♯
C/E
D
Em
I can fly high-
C
Em7
E7(♭9)
-er than an ea - gle,
Am
Am7/D
D7
To Coda
G
'cause you are the wind beneath my wings.
D. S. al Coda
C

3. It might have appeared to go unnoticed
that I've got it all here in my heart.
I want you to know I know the truth:
I would be nothing without you.

YOU LIGHT UP MY LIFE

Words and Music by
JOE BROOKS
Arranged by DAN COATES

You Light up My Life - 3 - 1

G
Gmaj7
G7
You light up my life. You give me
mf
E7
Am
Am7
hope to car - ry on. You light up my
D7
To Coda
G
Em
days and fill my nights with
1.
Am7
D
2.
Am7
D.S. al Coda
D7
song. song. 'Cause

Coda
B
B7
Em
nights
with
song.
cresc.
f
A7
G/D
B7
Em
It can't be wrong when it feels so right,
A7
G/D
D7sus4
D7
'cause you, you
mf
mp
C G D
C
G/B Am7
G
light up my life.
rit.
slower
mf

YOU MEAN THE WORLD TO ME

Words and Music by
L.A. REID, DARYL SIMMONS
and BABYFACE
Arranged by DAN COATES

Moderate, steady beat
mf
mp
B♭maj7
Am7
Dm
If you could
give me one good rea - son
gon - na take some work - in' but
why I should be - lieve you, be
I be - lieve you're worth it, as
lieve in all the - things that you tell.
long as your in - ten - tions are good.
I would
There is
sure like to be - lieve you, my
just one way to show it and
You Mean the World to Me - 6 - 1

Am7 D Gm7
heart wants to re - ceive you. Just make me know that you are sin - cere.
boy I hope you know it that no one could love you like I could.
C7 B♭maj7
You know I'd love for you to lead me and
Lord knows I wan - na trust you, and
Am7 Dm B♭maj7
fol - low through com - plete - ly, so won't you give me all I ask for.
ba - by, how I'd love you. I'm not sure that love is e - nough.
Am7 Dm B♭maj7
And if you give your ver - y best to
And I will not be for - sak - en, I

Am7 Ab7 Gm7
bring me hap - pi - ness, I'll show you just how much I a - dore
hope there's no mis - tak - in', so tell me that you'll al - ways be true.
C7 F
you. 'Cause you mean the world to me, you are my ev -
mf
F/Eb Dm
'ry - thing. I swear the on - ly thing that mat - ters,
Dbmaj7 Db6 F
mat - ters to me. Oh, ba - by, ba - by, ba - by, ba - by,

G/B
Gm7
D♭maj7
ba - by, 'cause you mean so much to me.
1.
B♭/C
2.
B♭/C
Now it's
There's a
Am7
Dm7
feel - ing in my heart that I know I can't es - cape, so
mf
Gm7
B♭/C
C/B♭
please don't let me go, don't let it be too late. There's a

A7
Dm7
time when words are good and they just get in the way. So
Gm7
show me how you feel, ba - by, I'm for real. Oh,
B♭/C
D♭maj7
C7
ba - by, ba - by, ba - by, ba - by. 'Cause you mean the world
cresc.
F
F/E♭
to me, you are my ev - 'ry - thing. I swear the on -
f

Dm
Db maj7
Db6
ly thing that mat - ters,
mat - ters to me.
Oh,
F
G/B
ba - by, ba - by, ba - by, ba - by,
ba - by,
'cause you mean so
Gm7
Gm7/C
1.
much to me.
'Cause you mean the world
2.
Gb maj7
Fmaj7
mp

THIS I PROMISE YOU

Words and Music by
RICHARD MARX
Arranged by DAN COATES

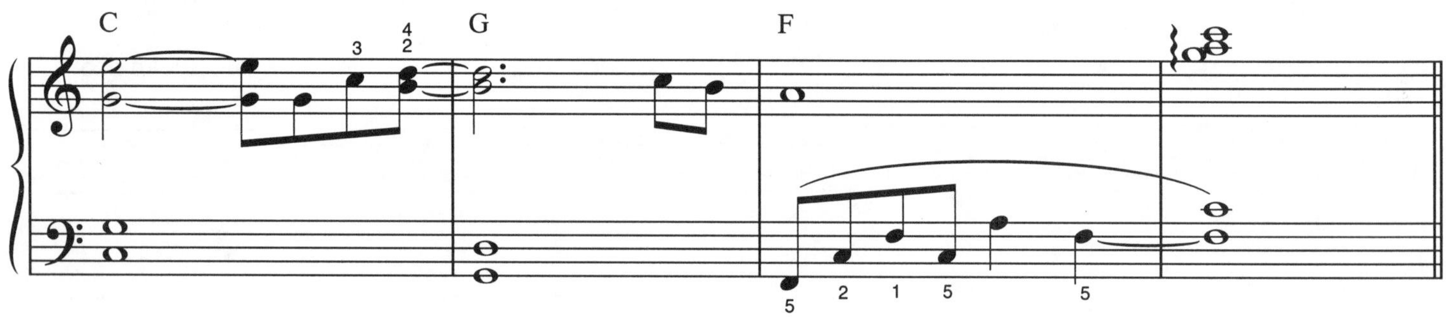

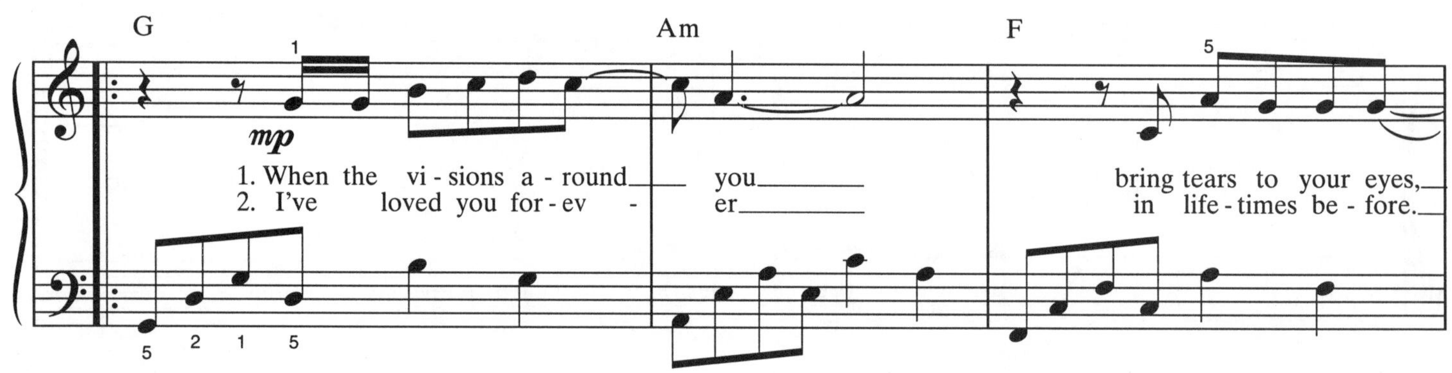

F G Dm7
are se-crets and lies, I'll be your strength,
will you hurt an-y-more. I give you my word. I
G7 C G/B Am
I'll give you hope, keep-ing your faith when it's gone. The
give you my heart. This is a bat-tle we've won. And
Dm7 Fm Gsus
one you should call was stand-ing here all a-long.
with this vow, for-ev-er has now be-gun.
G C G
And I will take you in my arms and
Just close your eyes each lov-ing day and
mf
Am F C/G
hold you right where you be-long.
know this feel-ing won't go a-way.
'Til the day my life is

1.
2.
G
F
C
Dm7
Gsus
D
A
Bm
mf
f
through, this I prom - ise you. This I prom - ise you.
ise you.
O - ver and o - ver I fall
when I hear you call.
With - out you in my life,
ba - by, I just would - n't be liv - ing at all.
And
I will take you in my arms and hold you right where you
close your eyes each lov - ing day and know this feel - ing won't go

1.
G
D/A
A
be - long.
a - way.
'Till the day my life is
Ev - 'ry word I say is
through, this I prom -
2.
G
A
G
ise you. Just
true, this I prom - ise you.
D
A
mf
Ev - 'ry word I say is
true, this I prom -
G
D
ise you.
dim.
Oh, I prom - ise you.
G/D
D
G/D
D
mp
rit.
p

SHEET MUSIC HITS

Chart-toppers at the Easy Piano Level! arr. by Dan Coates

Popular Sheet Music Hits
(AFM0313)

Titles include: As Time Goes By • Back at One • Because You Loved Me • Foolish Games • God Bless the U.S.A. • Greatest Love of All • I Could Not Ask for More • I Turn to You • I Will Always Love You • Lean on Me • My Way • Now and Forever • Over the Rainbow • The Prayer • The Rose • Somewhere Out There • Theme from New York, New York • There You'll Be • A Thousand Miles • Time to Say Goodbye • To Where You Are • Un-Break My Heart • The Wind Beneath My Wings • You Needed Me • Your Song.

Country Sheet Music Hits
(AFM0311)

Titles include: Amazed • Because You Love Me • Breathe • Come On Over • Concrete Angel • The Dance • From This Moment On • Go Rest High on That Mountain • Holes in the Floor of Heaven • How Do I Live • I Could Not Ask for More • I Cross My Heart • I Hope You Dance • I Swear • I'll Be • I'm Already There • I'm Movin' On • The Keeper of the Stars • On the Side of Angels • Something That We Do • There You Are • This Kiss • When You Say Nothing at All • You're Still the One.

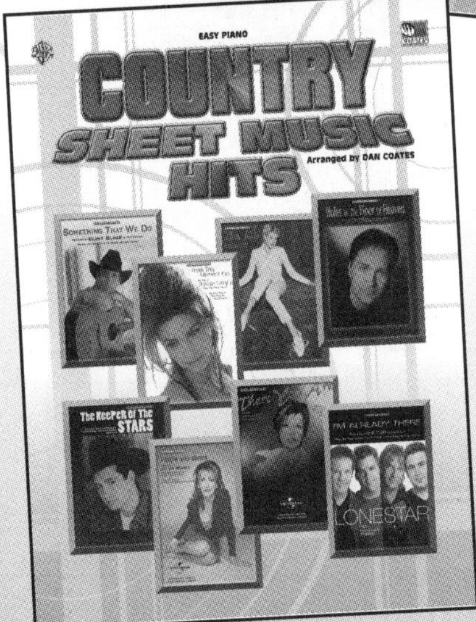

Wedding Sheet Music Hits
(AFM0312)

Titles include: All I Have • Always • Amazed • Because of You • Ave Maria (Schubert) • Endless Love • Bridal Chorus • At Last • Forever and for Always • From This Moment On • Here and Now • How Deep Is Your Love • I Swear • Love Like Ours • In Your Eyes • Once in a Lifetime • This Magic Moment • Tonight I Celebrate My Love • Wedding Song (There Is Love) • The Wedding March (from "A Midsummer Night's Dream") • With This Ring • Years from Here • You Light Up My Life • Your Love Amazes Me • You're the Inspiration.

Movie Music Sheet Music Hits
(AFM0316)

Titles include: Across the Stars • And All That Jazz • Arthur's Theme (The Best That You Can Do) • Because You Loved Me • Come What May • The Entertainer • Eye of the Tiger • Fawkes the Phoenix • Gollum's Song • Hedwig's Theme • How Do I Live • I Believe I Can Fly • I Don't Want to Miss a Thing • In Dreams • James Bond Theme • Over the Rainbow • Somewhere, My Love (Lara's Theme) • Somewhere Out There • Star Wars (Main Title) • Stayin' Alive • Tears in Heaven • That's What Friends Are For • Theme from Ice Castles (Through the Eyes of Love) • There You'll Be • The Wind Beneath My Wings.

TV Sheet Music Hits
(AFM0317)

Titles include: Ballad of Gilligan's Isle • The Batman Theme • Boss of Me • Charlie's Angels • Everybody Loves Raymond • Flying Without Wings • Hawaii Five-O • High Upon This Love • Hill Street Blues Theme • I'll Be There for You • Law and Order • Mighty Morphin Power Rangers • Movin' On Up • Peter Gunn Theme • The Pink Panther • Searchin' My Soul • Song from M*A*S*H • Theme from Family Guy • Theme from the Simpsons • This Is It! • This Is the Night • Those Were the Days • The West Wing • Where There Is Hope • Whose Line Is It Anyway? • WKRP in Cincinnati.

Broadway Sheet Music Hits
(AFM0315)

Titles include: Almost Like Being in Love • And All That Jazz • Beautiful City • Bewitched • Dancing Queen • Don't Cry for Me Argentina • Falling in Love with Love • Favorite Son • Heart • Hey There • How Could I Ever Know? • If My Friends Could See Me Now! • I'll Never Fall in Love Again • My Funny Valentine • No More • Ragtime • Send in the Clowns • Summertime • Sunrise, Sunset • Tenterfield Saddler • Thoroughly Modern Millie • What More Can I Say? • With a Song in My Heart • You Can Always Count on Me • You Took Advantage of Me.

Classic Rock Sheet Music Hits
(AFM0314)

Titles include: After Midnight • American Pie • Bad Moon Rising • Black Water • Brown Eyed Girl • Down on the Corner • Drive • Europa • Free Bird • Gimme Some Lovin' • Go Your Own Way • Heart of Gold • Higher Love • Hotel California • Layla • Long Train Runnin' • Lyin' Eyes • Maggie May • More Than a Feeling • Old Time Rock & Roll • Open Arms • Proud Mary • Sister Golden Hair • What a Fool Believes.

Collect All Seven Music-Packed Volumes!

AD1148 5/04